DON'T RENT BUY!

A Step-by-Step Guide to Buying Your First Home

EDDIE FADEL

DON'T RENT INC.
Oak Brook, Illinois

Don't Rent, Inc., P.O. Box 3245, Oak Brook, IL 60522
Visit our website at: www.dontrent.com

This book is for informational purposes only. It does not provide business, legal, tax, or investment advice and should not be relied on as such. Neither the author nor the publisher guarantees or warrants that the information in this book is accurate, complete, up to date, or will produce certain financial results or investment returns. The information is general in nature and may not apply to particular factual or legal circumstances. Individuals should consult their own business, legal, tax, or investment advisor for advice. The author and publisher make no warranty, expressed or implied, and assume no legal liability or responsibility for the accuracy, completeness, timeliness or usefulness of any information in this book.

ISBN: 978-0-9819128-0-6

Library of Congress Control Number: 2008935956

Printed in the United States of America
10 9 8 7 6 5 4 3 2

Cover design by Josh Bean
Cover photography by Omar Cruz
Interior design by www.tothepointsolutions.com

I dedicate this book to my family, my friends and my clients. I also want to recognize the dedicated real estate agents, brokers and REALTORS®, the honest, hardworking mortgage bankers, attorneys and title agents, and the high quality home builders I've had the honor of being associated with for so many years. I appreciate their confidence in me and I thank them for the opportunities I've had to work with each of them.

CONTENTS

PREFACE

I arrived in this country from my native Lebanon for the first time in 1987. The opportunity to actually own a house in my newly adopted country amazed me. It still does, more than 20 years later. No other country in the world makes it so easy to become a homeowner. **None.** No other country in the world bestows so many economic and intangible benefits to every homeowner, regardless of the size, location or price of the home. **None.** No other country in the world puts home ownership within the grasp of all its citizens. **None.**

We'll discuss some of the many programs for and benefits of home ownership later. But the fact is that millions of Americans—to my continuing bewilderment—have not taken advantage of the greatest financial and peace-of-mind opportunity available to them and their families. They continue to rent.

This book is intended to help you. In fact, it's my way of demanding that you take advantage of the unprecedented opportunities you have right now to become a homeowner!

As we go to press, I don't want you to be frightened by the past and present media coverage devoted to the real estate "bubble" of several years ago and subsequent events. Beneath that veneer of bad news, there is good news—and a lot of it—for first time homebuyers. Market conditions now and into the foreseeable future continue to favor home ownership over renting. These four factors are responsible:

1. **The inventory of homes on the market.** The real estate "bubble" that burst in 2008-2009 resulted in an unprecedented number of homes for sale all over the United States— a record 4 million! While that number has declined somewhat over the past several years, there are still more homes for sale than there are qualified buyers. That spells opportunity for you. New construction offers opportunity, too; a builder might reduce prices to close out a development, for example.

2. **The number of foreclosed homes on the market.** For more information about buying foreclosed, or real estate owned (REO) properties, make sure you read the Foreword: About Foreclosures and REOs, which follows.

3. **Mortgage loans are at historically low interest rates.** For example: 30-year fixed rate mortgages are in the low 4.0% range, with 15-year fixed rate mortgages in the mid-3.5% range. Five year adjustable rates are near 3.0%. For conforming loans mortgage money is available via any number of Freddie Mac, Fannie Mae, FHA, VA and other programs. (See chapters 2 and 9)

4. **The cost of renting a home continues its steady upward climb.** A convergence of negative economic conditions has forced many former or would-be homeowners out of the market, or kept them out, and they've had no choice but to rent. The result – rental rates have climbed. You can compare the real costs of renting versus buying using the charts and tools offered on the GinnieMae website at www.ginniemae.gov/rent_vs_buy.

This is an exceptionally favorable time to buy your first home, or to put yourself squarely on the path to first-time homeownership with the information you will read in the pages of this guide.

There is another factor involved, too. It's all about value. As I wrote earlier, I was amazed by the homeowning opportunities, advantages and possibilities available to Americans when I first came to this country. Almost three decades later, I'm still amazed at the values offered in the United States housing market, especially compared to similar residential properties in Europe, Asia and the Middle East. It is not uncommon as I write this in mid-2012 for three- and four-bedroom homes in the United States to be selling for a fraction of what their counterparts are costing abroad—right now! A three-bedroom house in virtually any metro-suburban area in the United States might sell for more than $250,000—while its counterpart in some markets abroad easily could cost a million dollars, or more!

So add another advantage to the list of reasons to buy now, rather than rent: outstanding value for your home-buying dollar.

Having said that, I want to tell you what this book is not. It's not a guide to buying a house, or houses, with no money down. It's not a technique that promises you thousands of dollars in monthly cash flow by over-leveraging rental properties into a fragile "house of cards." It's not a get rich quick scheme via real estate. If that's what you're looking for, don't waste your time.

This book has but one objective: to encourage and convince you to quit writing checks to your landlord! My message is simple: Don't Rent. And there is only one way to do that: Buy a home. Become a first-time home buyer.

Before you start thinking of all the reasons you can't do that, let me assure you of one fact: You are wrong. You can buy your own home. What's more, I'm telling you MUST buy your own home. It is in your best interests from every angle imaginable—financial, long-term, short term, family, retirement, you name it. Home ownership is essential to your long term financial health and to your family's well being now and into the future.

If you have suffered through the legally, financially and personally painful process of foreclosure, I want to tell you that you can become a homeowner again. Perhaps you bought at the peak of the market and for some reason could not sell the property at its depressed price. Perhaps you took on a sub-prime loan that saddled you with a high interest rate and a monthly mortgage that demanded far more of your income (some as high at 60%) than was prudent. Perhaps you lost your job, were divorced or were adversely affected by some other life-changing event.

To become a homeowner again, think of yourself as a first time buyer. In fact, if you've not owned a home in the last three years, you *are* considered to be a first time buyer. Either way, work on rebuilding your credit (see chapter 3) and settle your old debts as soon as possible. You can get a mortgage if your income is stable and you've rebuilt your credit. Most importantly, be realistic about what you can afford: Your monthly mortgage payment, including principal, interest, taxes, insurance (PITI) and any applicable home-owners' association fees, should range between 28-33% of your gross monthly income.

You must become a homeowner again and I know you can do it!

Is it easy? No. Whether you're re-entering the market or a first time homebuyer, this is a complicated, step-by-step and carefully considered process that you must be aware of as you go through it. You can master it if you read carefully, don't do anything you don't understand and enlist the help of competent and ethical professionals at every step along the way. Don't forget: Millions of people became first-time homeowners in the past couple of years. It can be done—and you can do it!

This book has ten chapters; I've written each as a guide to a specific task or responsibility that you must complete on the way to becoming a first-time homeowner. Read each one carefully and make ample use of all the information resources I've provided within the chapters, in the appendix at the end of the book and at my website, www.dontrent.com.

You can't know too much about home buying because, if you're like me and millions of other homeowners, it will be the largest purchase you'll ever make. So do yourself a favor as you begin the journey toward home ownership: learn as much as you can about the entire process.

With regard to learning as much as you can, two recent developments deserve your attention.

First, your credit score. It's more important than ever. It's altogether possible that you will be unable to get a loan if your credit score is not at least—and I emphasize *at least*—620. Chapter 3 tells you how to obtain copies of your credit report at no cost. More information is available at http://www.federalreserve.gov/creditreports/. Before you seek pre-approval for your mortgage, visit that site.

Second, recent federal legislation has created the Nationwide Mortgage Licensing System & Registry (NMLS). You can access the site at http://mortgage.nationwidelicensingsystem.org. It's a free service to confirm that the mortgage company or mortgage professional with whom you want to conduct business is authorized to conduct mortgage business in your state. Go to the site and click on "Consumer Access".

During my career in the mortgage industry, I've been extremely fortunate. I've helped buyers with sterling credit histories and ample down payments buy their first homes. And I'm proud to say I've helped buyers with weak credit histories rebuild their credit, bring their personal finances under control and become homeowners. It's been a joy, and a source of great personal satisfaction, to see them realize the myriad of advantages that every first-time homeowner enjoys, regardless of the location, size or price of the house they bought!

The common thread among all of them? They made a commitment to own their homes. They decided to quit writing monthly checks to their landlords. They followed my advice: Don't Rent!

I want to say the same thing about you.

Eddie Fadel
June, 2012

ACKNOWLEDGMENTS

So many people contributed to the success of this publication, from giving me encouragement about writing it when it was just an idea to helping make sure I stayed the course and saw it through to publication.

I want to acknowledge with deep appreciation the special efforts of:

Joe Bean, for his editorial contributions;

Sandra Carone, for her earlier editorial contributions;

Alex Spencer and Thomas Kaput, for their meticulous attention to detail and accuracy.

And I want to express my gratitude and admiration to all of you whose knowledge, dedication, sense of service and devotion to the highest standards of ethical conduct continue to make first-time home ownership a reality for millions of deserving Americans. You are the inspiration for this book.

About Foreclosed And REO Properties

The foreclosure process is not within the scope of this book. However, it is possible for you to buy a home out of foreclosure. I want to give you some basic information—and it is intentionally *very* basic—if you want to consider this avenue to first time home ownership. Laws governing the foreclosure process vary from state to state, so I'm not going to discuss the legal issues involved in foreclosure. You must have an attorney review all documents relating to the property to make sure the title is clear and that there are no legal impediments at the time of purchase or later.

"**Foreclosure** is the procedure by which a party who has loaned money secured by a mortgage or deed of trust on real property (or has an unpaid judgment), forces the sale of the real property to recover the money due, unpaid interest, plus the costs of foreclosure, after the debtor fails to make payment."[1]

What that means, of course, has become painfully evident in the last several years. Homeowners who have been unable to make their

---

1. www.uslegal.com

regular mortgage payments have been forced to sell their homes under duress or to vacate them

I do not recommend buying a home out of foreclosure **if** your intention is to do minor repairs and **"flip" it**—put it back on the market for quick and, you hope, profitable sale. Foreclosed homes that have been empty for some time—several months or more—are susceptible to deterioration through a lack of routine maintenance, plumbing or heating failures and other causes.

Sooner or later, these homes will be put on the market, either by the distressed owner, at auction by the lender, or by the lender who has taken title to the property.

You can buy a home in foreclosure at one of three points in the process. While each of the three has some advantages, I believe that you are in the most favorable position as a first time buyer when you can negotiate directly with the lender on the purchase of Real Estate Owned (REO). Therefore, if you are interested in buying a foreclosed home, I suggest you ask your agent to focus on REO properties.

Here is a brief outline of the three ways to buy an about-to-be foreclosed or foreclosed house:

1. You can buy a home that's in the ***pre-foreclosure phase***. This means the borrower has missed from one to four payments or more (remember—state laws vary widely!) and has been notified by the lender that the foreclosure process has begun. In this instance, you can buy the property from the homeowner with the approval of the mortgagee. Ask your real estate agent to let the owner or lender know you're interested in the property. Usually, you will have some time for your attorney to research the title and you will be able to inspect the property, or have a professional conduct a home inspection for you. If your purchase price is less than the amount owed on the mortgage, the transaction can be called a short sale.

2. A home that's been foreclosed upon can be **purchased at a public auction**. You will be required to bid competitively on the property, and it's possible you will be required to pay cash. While this avoids the necessity of dealing with the owner or lender, or both, bidding at auction gives you little, if any, time to research the title, or to conduct a thorough property inspection—if any.

3. The third avenue to home ownership through the foreclosure process is to **buy directly from the owner**—the lender. In this phase, the lender has assumed ownership of the property; it's usually referred to as REO—Real Estate Owned. The lender will be seeking the highest price in its attempt to sell the home and might, or might not, be willing to make needed repairs or other concessions to make the home more attractive. You can expect to negotiate the purchase price and other details with the lender, just as you would in a more traditional real estate transaction.

With these three options available to you, and with the differences in state laws affecting the entire purchase process, I strongly urge you to work with a professional real estate agent who is an expert on buying foreclosed properties. See chapter 5 for a complete discussion about how to find an agent.

Regardless of where in the process you find what you believe to be an acceptable balance between risk and opportunity, I remind you: Buying a home at any point in foreclosure is complex and can be unpredictable. In some states, for example, the former owner can redeem (recover) the property, even after it's been sold.

So I repeat: work with an experienced real estate agent expert in dealing with foreclosed properties. Utilize the services of an experienced real estate attorney. You can learn more about foreclosures at www.hud.gov.

Now, let's get to work on getting you ready to become a first time homebuyer.

Don't Rent Buy!

1

Introduction to Homeownership

Personal and Financial Advantages

If you really want to own your own home, keep reading! I don't want you to rent—I want to help you to become a homeowner. If you read this book and follow my suggestions, you can be in your own home much sooner than you think.

Did your landlord raise the rent again this year? Did you see some or most of your annual pay raise go right to your landlord? Chances are the mortgage payment you're making for your landlord didn't increase this year—so why should your rent? Sure, you have some alternatives. You can move to another house or apartment, but moving is expensive. It takes a lot of time to find another place. Packing is time consuming. And moving is disruptive, especially for a family with children.

Maybe your rent hasn't changed. If you want to exercise your creative talents and decorate your kid's room, you're going to need your landlord's permission before you do. If you owned your own home, you could do what you—and your kids—want. You could remodel or renovate without anyone's permission. You would be in charge of your home because you own it.

So instead of putting your hard-earned salary or bonus into your landlord's bank account, you could add as many personal touches to your own home as you want. You might even get a return on your investment if you choose to sell your property.

> "... the financial advantages of home ownership far outweigh any benefits (beyond a convenience here and there) to renting."

Home ownership has all kinds of financial advantages, as you will learn from reading this book. It's not a one-way street, of course. Being a renter has some advantages—having little responsibility for repairs and upkeep being the most obvious. If you have a leaky faucet or the garbage disposal quits working at your rental home, you simply call your landlord. Your landlord sends out a service person to fix the problem and it costs you nothing.

On the other hand, when you're a homeowner, it's your job to repair that leaky faucet or malfunctioning garbage disposal.

I'm saying "don't rent!" and I'm urging you to buy a home because the financial advantages of home ownership far outweigh any benefits (beyond a convenience here and there) to renting. For example, owning your own home means:

→ Your monthly payment won't increase with a fixed rate mortgage

→ The value of your house customarily will increase over time

→ You enjoy the considerable benefits of important tax advantages available only to homeowners

→ You will save money, directly (your mortgage payment can be less than your rent) or indirectly (considering the tax advantages of home ownership)

Let's take a look at each of these financial advantages in greater detail.

Fixed Mortgage Payments

As you continue to make payments to the principal, the outstanding balance of the mortgage is reduced. This becomes a forced savings to you because, over time, your equity will increase. And even a modest rate of inflation, over time, means that you will be paying an old, fixed-rate debt with cheaper dollars. As a renter, you have no opportunity to build equity, regardless of the size of the rental check you write every month. Your rent will increase over time, too—with no benefit to you. I think it's safe to assume that your rent increases will keep pace with—or out pace—the rate of inflation.

"As a renter, you have no opportunity to build equity, regardless of the size of the rental check you write every month."

If you obtain a fixed-rate mortgage on your home, the principal and interest portions of the loan remain the same year after year. Your monthly payment for a fixed-rate mortgage never goes up.[1] If you are renting, you can expect an increase in your monthly rent over time.

House Value Increases

Most homes increase in value over a period of time due to inflation. This increase is called appreciation. When your home appreciates, it adds to your equity. The longer you stay in your home, on average, the more it is worth. Many people see their homes as an investment for the future. They plan retirement around its value. Other people plan to pay for their children's college tuition with the equity they accumulate in their homes.

Tax Benefits

At the end of each year, your lender is required to provide Form 1098 to you. The form shows the total amount of interest you paid on your home loan during the preceding year. As a home owner, you can deduct mortgage interest and property tax when you file your personal income tax returns. You also can deduct some costs associated with your mortgage and, in some cases, moving expenses related to your job. I'm not a tax accountant or CPA, so please consult with your tax adviser or tax return preparer for up to date and complete information.

Your House as your Savings Account

Many first-time homebuyers usually don't have enough cash to purchase a home without borrowing from a lender. It's hard enough to save money for a down payment! The down payment is your

> ## "Many people see their homes as an investment for the future."

---

1. You may incur minimal increases in your property tax and insurance portions of your mortgage payment only.

equity in the property; equity is the positive difference between the value of the property and what is still owed on the house. For example:

Cost of your House	$200,000
Subtract your Down Payment	- 20,000 (equity)
Mortgage	$180,000

When you buy a house, you make monthly mortgage payments to the lender. Part of a monthly mortgage payment pays the interest you owe the lender for financing your home. The remainder of your payment goes towards the principal each month. The principal is the amount of money you borrowed to buy your house.

Other Advantages

Another financial advantage of homeownership is being able to use the equity you have in the property without selling it. Here's an example: The original purchase price of your home was $200,000 and you made a 20% down payment. Your mortgage payments over the past ten years have reduced your outstanding loan amount to $120,000. Your house is now worth $250,000. You have $130,000 in equity: present value ($250,000)—total owed ($120,000) = $130,0000.

You don't have to own your home "free and clear" to tap into this value. If you need cash, you can take out a second mortgage or open a line of credit based on the equity you have in your home.

A second mortgage loan can be used for a specific purpose and must be for an exact amount of money. It is repayable over a fixed period of time. Your property serves as the security for the loan. The interest rate on a second mortgage is higher than the first mortgage, and in most cases, lower than you would pay for a personal loan.

A home equity loan, which means you're borrowing from yourself, usually allows you to qualify for a line of credit at lower interest rates. Because the debt is secured by your home, all or part of the interest paid on the home equity loan can be tax deductible. Check with your accountant or tax preparer.

Ready or Not?

That's a brief introduction to some of the many personal and financial advantages of owning a home.

At the very least, I hope I have you thinking about *why* you're renting. At best, I've convinced you that buying a home is so much better than renting that you're ready to begin the process by telling yourself: Don't Rent!

I'd like to help you determine if you are ready for homeownership now—or if you need to take action in your personal life now so you can start getting ready to buy your first home soon.

Are you Financially Ready?

Do you pay your bills on time? Are your credit card balances at a minimum? Do you put money into a savings account regularly? These are just some of the important questions you'll be asked when you consider buying a house.

Create a Budget

Now is the time to take a look at your spending habits. Do you have any idea what you spend your money on each month? Is there any money left over at the end of each pay period? Unless you can answer a resounding "yes" to both those questions, it's time to develop a financial plan.

Start by tracking all your expenses to account for every penny of income and every penny you spend—every day—for 90 days. You can do this manually or you can buy an inexpensive personal money management computer program that will help you automate the process.

Start good record keeping habits if you don't already have them. Create a system to save all of your monthly statements in an organized manner, such as in labeled file folders or envelopes. I suggest you look at computerized home bookkeeping or budgeting programs that will help you capture and organize this information. When you are ready to buy a home, your lender will want to know how much debt you are obligated to pay each month; this is the first step in gathering that information.

> **"Your objective is to establish a budget, which can be a road map for you to get out of debt . . ."**

Your objective is to establish a budget, which can be a road map for you to get out of debt, or it can help you identify, set and meet financial goals. One financial goal? Saving enough money for a down payment on your first home.

If you are married, it's a good idea to track your expenses with your spouse. Creating a budget together and having common financial goals is important for success.

The first thing you will need to do is to take a look at your housing expenses. Housing expenses include your rent payment and the utilities you pay for which are not included in your rent, such as gas, electric, water and sewer bills.

Track Non-Housing Expenses

Next, collect information on non-housing expenses. Non-housing expenses include just about everything else, such as food, telephone, entertainment, day care, vacations, car payments, credit card payments, clothes and other things you buy.

Focus on your non-housing expenses. You can trim in this area if you want to save money for your down payment. Or, you might decide that credit card debt is eating up too much of your monthly income. If that's the case, I want to help you develop a plan to reduce that debt so you can achieve your financial goals sooner.

> **"Focus on your non-housing expenses. You can trim in this area if you want to save money . . ."**

Let's get started by first taking a look at your current monthly expenses and then at your monthly income. Use your bank statements, cancelled checks, cash receipts and other records to track these expenses. It's time to make some decisions on what to do with your earnings!

Track Monthly Expenses

Look over the identified Housing Expenses and the Non-Housing Expenses on the Monthly Expense Tracking Worksheet that follows. You may need to add categories that apply to you. Remember these are "monthly" expenses. So, make sure you total all bills that apply within a category and write the "total" monthly cost in the appropriate space.

For Example:

→ Under Housing Expenses you will see the Utilities category

→ Sub-categories for Utilities are gas, electric, water, and sewer

→ Add together the current month's bills for each sub-category

→ Write the total monthly dollar amount for all utilities in the Monthly Costs $ space provided.

Add the Housing and Non-Housing Monthly Costs Totals together and write that dollar amount in the Total Monthly Housing Expense space provided.

Monthly Expense Tracking Worksheet

Housing Expenses	Monthly Costs	✓
Rent	$	
Utilities (gas, electric, water, sewer)	$	
Total Monthly Housing Expenses	$	

Non-Housing Expenses	Monthly Costs	✓
Food (Groceries, dining out—dinner and lunches)	$	
Clothing Allowance (family)	$	
Telephone (Cell Phone(s), Land Line(s), Long Distance)	$	
Children (Daycare, Tuition, Activities, Allowances, Haircuts, etc.)	$	
Elder Care	$	
Cars (Loan Payments, Maintenance, Repairs, Insurance, Vehicle Stickers, Gasoline)	$	
Transportation (Bus, Taxi, etc.)	$	
Credit Card Payments	$	
Student Loans	$	
Installment Loans	$	

Entertainment	$	
Taxes Borrower 1	$	
Taxes Co-Borrower	$	
Insurance (other than car)	$	
Payroll Deductions Borrower 1	$	
Payroll Deductios Co-Borrower	$	
Total Monthly Non-Housing Expenses	$	
Total Monthly Housing and Non-Housing Expenses	$	

Analyzing your actual monthly income and your spending habits will tell you if you are spending more than you earn now, if you have the ability to save more money, or if you are already in a good position to buy a new home.

Remember, you will have to budget for expenses that go along with home ownership, such as property taxes and maintenance, you don't pay as a renter.

Analyze your Monthly Income

Next, review your Monthly Expense Tracking Worksheet (from the previous pages) and your Monthly Income Worksheet (on the next few pages).

Add or delete any categories for your own needs.

List all current, regular monthly income for yourself (Borrower 1) and anyone else who would be considered a borrower (Co-borrower 2), such as your spouse or significant other.

Include all sources of income during the past 12 months IF you will continue to have that income for at least three more years.

Monthly Income Worksheet

Borrower #1

Monthly gross income or salary	$
Overtime/Part-time/ Seasonal/ Commission income	$
Bonuses/Tips	$
Unemployment Compensation	$
Pension/Social Security Benefits	$
Veterans Administration Benefits	$
Public Assistance	$
Alimony/child support/separate maintenance income	$
	$
	$
Total Monthly Income	$

Co-Borrower #2

Monthly gross income or salary	$
Overtime/Part-time/ Seasonal/ Commission income	$
Bonuses/Tips	$
Unemployment Compensation	$
Pension/Social Security Benefits	$
Veterans Administration Benefits	$
Public Assistance	$
Alimony/child support/separate maintenance income	$
	$
	$
Total Monthly Income	$

→ Add the Total Monthly Income from Borrower #1 and Co-Borrower #2 and write that total on line 1 below.

→ Write your Total Monthly Expenses form Worksheet #1 on line 2 below.

→ Then, subtract line 2 from line 1 below and write that amount (negative or positive) on line 3.

1. Total Monthly Income $_____

2. Total Monthly Expenses $_____

3. Negative (-) or Positive (+) Total $_____

If your income (line #1) is greater than your expenses (line #2), I commend you! If you have a savings account with enough money in it to pay for the down payment on a house, plus your settlement costs, moving expenses, and other necessary items, congratulations! Skip the next few paragraphs and move on to the next chapter, *What does it Cost to Buy a Home?*

However, if your expenses (line #2) are greater than your income (line #1), it's time to revisit Monthly Expense Worksheet #1 on the previous pages.

Perhaps that payroll deduction item should represent a savings account to save money for a down payment. Or you might want to put money towards credit card debt instead of paying the minimum balance. How about working towards paying off installment loans or student loans?

Now is the time to decide if you are really committed to that American Dream . . . homeownership! If you're still hanging in here with me, place a check mark next to the non-housing expenses you plan to reduce or eliminate.

Example:

Non-Housing Expenses	Monthly Costs	✓
Food (Groceries, dining out—dinner and lunches)	$	
Clothing Allowance (family)	$	
Telephone (Cell Phone(s), Land Line(s), Long Distance)	$	

Tracking your expenses, reducing your debt, and saving money are the first steps in seeing if you are financially prepared to own a home. If you're wondering just how much money you'll need to save, keep reading. I'm confident that I can say . . . DON'T RENT . . . because you can buy!

Let's take a look at chapter two to learn more.

2

What Does it Cost to Buy a Home?

Where will all that money come from?

Remember, I never said this was going to be easy! Buying a home costs money—upfront expenses, your down payment, closing costs, settling-in costs, and expenditures that go beyond your purchase. Once you're in your new home, you'll have your monthly mortgage payment, taxes, insurance, utility bills, and more.

Right about now, you might be thinking I'm crazy for saying "DON'T RENT!" You might be wondering how you'll ever be able to afford all these expenses unless you increase your income significantly, and that doesn't usually happen overnight.

Don't worry. I'm going to tell you about the many different types of financing options that can help you achieve your dream of home-ownership. I know you can do it and I want to help you buy. Remember my message to you: DON'T RENT!

Financing Options

Private and government sponsored programs are available to first time homebuyers, low-income families, the elderly, and individuals with disabilities, minority families, and more.

I'll review these loan options in greater detail in Chapter 9, where I will provide you with the information needed to help you select the best mortgage solution for your financial situation. At a minimum, I want you to be aware of the loan programs designed to assist millions of Americans like you in meeting your housing needs.

If any of the financing options you read about apply to you, and if you meet the standard requirements for specific programs, you may be able to achieve the American Dream of homeownership sooner than you think! So . . . DON'T RENT! You can buy!

Upfront Costs

Let's take a quick look at some of the upfront costs and ongoing expenses you'll need to be aware of before you consider purchasing a home.

You must pay three upfront costs when you buy a house:

→ The down payment

→ Closing costs

→ Moving and settling costs

The Down Payment

As we discussed earlier, the lender regards your down payment as your financial interest in the house. It is a required sum of money you must contribute as part of the mortgage and it's the lender's security that you will repay the loan.

Traditionally, private lenders require a down payment of at least

20 percent of the purchase price of the house—meaning that a $200,000 house requires a $40,000 down payment. Because 20 percent of the purchase price can be a substantial sum of money for a first time homebuyer to save, I want you to make you aware of several borrowing options which require down payments of less than the traditional 20 percent.

Low Down Payment Mortgage Solutions

Low down payment mortgage programs available to first time homebuyers operate under the guidelines of private and government agencies.

Private lenders provide consumers with conventional mortgage programs governed by Federal National Mortgage Association (Fannie Mae) and Federal Home Loan Mortgage Corporation (Freddie Mac) guidelines. These guidelines help private lenders decide whether a borrower is willing and able to repay the mortgage on time and whether the property is valuable enough to help pay off the mortgage if the borrower defaults on the payments.

Fannie Mae offers no- to low down payment mortgage programs if you:

→ Need greater flexibility with regard to your credit history and if you are a full time primary or secondary education employee, police officer, or firefighter

→ Purchase qualified energy-efficient housing.

→ Use 3 percent of your own personal funds plus:

→ 2 percent "gift" from a family member (with no pay back terms)

OR

→ 2 percent grant or loan from a non-profit organization, state, or local government agency

→ Have limited funds for your down payment and closing costs[1]

→ Need a greater amount of your monthly income toward housing costs compared to other standard mortgage products[2]

→ Have limited cash resources and need flexible credit guidelines (various mortgage solutions are available)

Freddie Mac makes low down payment mortgage programs available to homebuyers, such as:

→ No down payment for borrowers with exceptional credit

→ 3 percent down payment for borrowers with good credit

→ 5 percent down payment for borrowers with past credit record blemishes

→ 3 percent and 5 percent down payment options for low and moderate income borrowers with alternative credit needs

→ Mortgages with secondary financing using a variety of mortgage products to create the 20 percent down payment

Government Agencies

The Federal Housing Administration (FHA) administers an insurance program that protects private individuals and institutions that lend money. The lender is protected against monetary loss if the homeowner doesn't make payments toward the money borrowed. The homebuyer achieves homeownership by obtaining relatively low down payment loans and long-term mortgages.

HUD/FHA

An FHA insured loan, which has flexible guidelines for qualification, will allow you to purchase a home with a low down payment.

Without provisions for income limits or credit scoring, an FHA loan is possible for borrowers who can afford the monthly mortgage payments and have reasonable credit histories.

The down payment requirement for an FHA insured loan is low in contrast to a non-conforming[3] or sub-prime[4] mortgage program, which frequently requires a larger down payment. Single-family home mortgages insured by FHA under Section 203(b) make it possible to reduce down payments for borrowers to as little as 3.5 percent of the purchase price. .

An FHA-acceptable down payment is unique because it can be a 100% gift to the borrower from a family member, relative or charitable organization.

Ginnie Mae

Ginnie Mae, the Government National Mortgage Association (GNMA), helps ensure that mortgage funds are available throughout the United States, including rural and urban areas where traditionally it has been more difficult to borrow money to buy a home. The Ginnie Mae guaranty is backed by the full faith and credit of the United States.

Mortgages are insured by the Federal Housing Administration (FHA), or by the Rural Housing Service (RHS), or the Department of Veterans Affairs (VA)[5] guarantees them.

Department Of Veterans Affairs

For active duty or retired military personnel, some members of the military reserve and National Guard, the VA Home Loan Program offers products and benefits to individuals who have served or are serving our nation.

The VA allows a veteran whose income and credit qualifies him or her to purchase a primary residence without a down payment. The sales price cannot exceed the appraised value of the home.

VA loans offer:

→ Equal opportunity for all qualified veterans to obtain a VA loan.

→ No down payment (unless required by the lender or the purchase price is more than the reasonable value of the property).

→ Buyer informed of reasonable value.

→ Negotiable interest rate.

→ Ability to finance the VA funding fee (plus reduced funding fees with a down payment of at least 5% and exemption for veterans receiving VA compensation).

→ Closing costs are comparable with other financing types (and may be lower).

→ No mortgage insurance premiums.

→ An assumable mortgage.

→ Right to prepay without penalty.

→ For homes inspected by VA during construction, a warranty from builder and assistance from VA to obtain cooperation of builder.

→ VA assistance to veteran borrowers in default due to temporary financial difficulty.

The Rural Housing Service (RHS) provides financing to farmers and other qualified borrowers buying property in rural areas who are unable to obtain loans elsewhere. Funds are borrowed from the U.S. Treasury.

RHS Single Family Housing loan programs might be of use if you're interested in buying a single family home in rural America.

To summarize this brief discussion of what's required with respect to your down payment: Don't stop looking because you don't have the money to make the traditional 20% down payment on the home of your dreams. Review the programs I've mentioned in detail; in my experience, you qualify for at least one of the programs I've listed. For more information, please see the appendix.

Closing Costs

Here's a brief recap:

Private/Conventional Loans: With most conventional loans, the borrower must pay closing costs equivalent to 2-3 percent of the price of the home at the time the sale closes.

FHA Loans: Many of the closing charges the borrower incurs with an FHA loan can be paid by seller concession—up to 3 percent of the purchase price. This reduces the cash-at-closing costs.

FHA rules impose limits on some fees lenders can charge when making a loan. For example, the loan origination fee charged by the lender for the administrative cost of processing the loan may not exceed one percent of the amount of the mortgage.

VA Loans: Veterans need money towards closing costs and the earnest money deposit, which is required by the seller when a sales contract is signed. Veterans may want to consider negotiating closing costs when a sales contract is being considered. The seller can pay for the costs of closing.

Settling-In Costs

Settling into a new home can generate expenses that creep up on you. Decide before you close on the house if you will need to buy a stove, refrigerator, washer, dryer or other essential appliance. Or you might need to make immediate repairs. (We'll talk about how to acquire and evaluate that information in chapter 8.) And don't forget the cost of moving into your new home—you might hire professional movers or rent a move-yourself truck or trailer.

Ongoing Costs

If you're still committed to becoming a homeowner, and I hope you are, I must tell you this: As a homeowner, you'll have to pay bills you've never had, such as your monthly mortgage payment, mortgage insurance (if the lender requires insurance), property taxes, homeowners insurance, utilities, and maintenance on the home. If you purchase a condominium, co-op, or townhouse, it's likely you will have a monthly homeowners association fee or other expenses.

Remember: Don't Rent!

> "The long-term financial and intangible benefits of homeownership far outweigh the additional expenses."

The long-term financial and intangible benefits of homeownership far outweigh the additional expenses. And remember that when you're buying your home, you're building equity. When you rent, you're paying for your landlord's real estate investment. As I've said before and as I'll say again and again: Don't Rent!

Ready or Not?

Now that you understand the personal and financial advantages of owning a home, have a handle on your current monthly expenses and understand where or if you need to cut costs, reduce debt and save money, I hope you're ready for homeownership now! If not, you can get there in the near future with a little determination and discipline in spending.

The rest of this book will guide you through all the steps in the process for obtaining the American Dream..homeownership. Each chapter will be based on one step of the Home Buying Checklist.

Home Buyer's Checklist	✓
Get Pre-Approved	
Prepare a Wish List/Choose a Location	
Find an Agent	
Look for a Home	
Negotiate the Purchase	
Hire an Inspector	
Obtain a Mortgage	
Close the Deal	

My goal is to make you a smart first time homebuyer who doesn't get surprised along the way.

I hope you'll take my advice: DON'T RENT! Become a home-owner as soon as you possibly can. Let's see what's next on this exciting journey.

Chapter Notes

1. 3% down payment required if you meet specific criteria.

2. 5% down payment required if you meet specific criteria.

3. Non-conforming mortgage product: A loan that does not meet the guidelines of Fannie Mae, Freddie Mac, or FHA.

4. Sub-prime mortgage product: A loan to assist borrowers who fall into a high-risk category. (The higher the risk, the higher the rate.)

5. www.va.gov

3

It's Time to Get Pre-Approved

What do I do now?

Before you start looking at houses, you need to establish the price range that's appropriate to your budget. You know what you can spend on housing each month, based on the expense worksheet you completed in Chapter 1. How much money you can borrow depends, in part, on how much you can repay on a monthly basis. The other determining factor is the size of your down payment. Together, they will determine the price range of the house you can buy.

Home Buying Checklist	✓
Get Pre-Approved	✓
Prepare a Wish List/ Choose a Location	
Find an Agent	
Look for a Home	
Negotiate the Purchase	
Hire an Inspector	
Obtain a Mortgage	
Close the Deal	

But how does the amount you can pay monthly translate to a purchase price?

In this chapter, I want to tell you what kind of guidelines lenders use to determine how much money you're qualified to borrow.

Pre-approve or Pre-qualify?

Based on financial information you provide, your real estate agent can calculate a maximum figure to help define the price range of homes you can afford. This pre-qualifying determines how much you are qualified to borrow from a lender based on preliminary questions. Pre-qualification provides a guideline for house hunting, but it does not say you are pre-approved for a mortgage.

So your first step in successful house-shopping is to get pre-approved for a loan. You gain a number of important advantages when you're pre-approved:

→ Pre-approval helps alleviate concerns a seller might have about your ability to get a loan. It tells the seller you qualify for a mortgage based on your credit history, financial and employment information.

→ Pre-approved buyers have more bargaining power because the seller knows you are a serious and able buyer.

→ Sellers are more willing to accept an offer from a pre-approved buyer.

To get pre-approved for a mortgage, you will complete a preliminary application process through a lender or a mortgage broker, or you can apply for pre-approval via the Internet. You will need a pre-approval letter from the source; it should state that you qualify for a mortgage for a specific sum of money. The letter should state that your credit is satisfactory.

Lending Professionals

Before you go through the pre-approval process, let's take a quick look at the differences between a mortgage lender and a mortgage broker. We'll also look at some of the advantages and disadvantages of using the Internet to obtain financing for your first home.

Lender

A lender is the supplier of the money, such as a bank, a savings and loan, a mortgage banker, or a credit union. If you choose to go directly to the lender for a loan, you can get only the loan products available through that lender. If the lender you chose does not have the type of loan you want, or need, you will need to look for another lender whose products meet your needs. It may take you weeks to find the right lender with the right loan products. However, if you are satisfied with the mortgage products offered, the rates, and the lender's closing costs, the lender can initiate and approve the loan, and issue the funds to close.

Mortgage Broker

On the other hand, a mortgage broker shops all the markets for you and originates the loan. Originating a loan means the mortgage broker working with you helps you gather all the documentation required to verify the financial information necessary for a loan. This can include employment and income verification, along with information about the source or sources of the cash you will be using for your down payment and closing costs. Acting on your behalf, the mortgage broker submits the paper work to a lender for approval. The broker does not lend money to you but serves as the link between you and a lender.

The advantage to you? The mortgage broker has access to different loan products offered by an array of lenders. If you don't qualify for a loan with one lender, the mortgage broker can move your application quickly to another lender with different requirements.

Internet Banking

Banking over the Internet is not much different than banking with a direct lender or mortgage broker. Generally, the same types of loan products your direct lender or mortgage broker has to offer are available online. Once you select an online lender and choose a loan you want, all you have to do is type away!

The advantage of using the Internet is that you can get pre-approved and apply for a mortgage without leaving your house. It's important for you to understand the various types of loan product offerings and which one will be best for you before you submit your online application. Most lenders' Internet sites will provide educational tools to help learn about different financing options. It's up to you to figure out what best suits your needs.

The disadvantage of using the Internet for first-time home buying is that you can miss the opportunity for guidance from an experienced professional in selecting the loan most appropriate to your needs. However, most Internet banking sites provide a phone number for you to call with questions.

Qualifying Guidelines

Whether you use a lender, a broker, or the Internet to get pre-approved for your mortgage, here are two "rules of thumb" that will help determine the amount of the mortgage you can expect:

→ Your monthly housing costs should total *no more than 28 percent* of your gross monthly income (before taxes). Monthly housing costs include: mortgage payment, property taxes, insurance, and condominium or cooperative fee (if applicable).

→ Your monthly housing costs plus other long-term debts

should *total no more than 36 percent* of your gross monthly income. Long-term debt is defined as financial obligations you have that will not be eliminated within the next ten months.

I want you to know there are mortgage products with different qualifying guidelines available to homebuyers that meet specific criteria. These products help borrowers qualify for mortgages with less income or a down payment lower than the traditional 20 percent. I will review these mortgage programs in Chapter 9.

What Lenders Look For

Your annual income, current interest rates, and your existing debt will help determine the amount of money you can borrow.

Income

A quick way to calculate the price range for you to purchase a home is to multiply your annual gross income (the amount you earn before taxes) by 2.5. Other factors will determine the exact amount of money you qualify for, such as your long-term debt and your credit history.

You can consider a co-purchaser's annual gross income if you are buying a house together with someone else, such as your spouse, a sibling or significant other. In that case, you will need to consider your co-purchaser's debt and credit history as well as your own.

Pre-Approval

1. Income

2. Employment History

3. Interest Rates/Terms

4. Debt/Good Credit

Employment History

In addition to these income requirements, lenders want you to have a steady job of at least two continuous years or more. It's OK if you have held more than one job for the two-year period, as long as the job move was for equal or greater pay. If you have worked less than two years, you will need to have a good reason for the gap in employment history and be able to explain the reason to the mortgage lender.

Examples of good reasons are:

→ Recently discharged from the military

→ Just finished school

→ Lay off due to the economy and lack of business for your company

In Chapter 1, you completed a Monthly Income Worksheet for you and a co-borrower. Revisit those worksheets to make sure you've included all the regular sources of income you have, such as veteran's benefits, interest income and child support.

Example:

If you and your co-purchaser's total gross annual income =

$50,000 + $50,000 = $100,000

Multiply the total ($100,000) times 2.5 = $250,000

In this example, you and your co-purchaser should consider homes costing $250,000 or less.

Remember, however, that lenders require a down payment on the purchase of a home. So the amount of money you save for your down payment can determine the size of your mortgage. Let's assume you qualify for a 5 percent down payment mortgage product in our example.

Example:

Purchase price	$250,000
5% down payment	12,500
Mortgage amount	$237,500

In this example, you will need to borrow $237,500 to purchase that home with the $250,000 price tag.

Don't forget the Lender's Qualifying Guideline: Your *monthly* housing costs (including mortgage payments, property taxes, and insurance and condominium or cooperative fee, if applicable) should total no more than 28 percent of your gross monthly income (before taxes). Lenders use the acronym PITI to described this sum; its stands for principal, interest, taxes and insurance.

I emphasize this fact: the more cash you put down on your home purchase, or the greater the investment you have in the property, the more lenient the lender is on the 28 percent qualifying ratio. If you are required to put 5 percent down on your home and that's what you do, expect your lender to stand firm on the 28 percent ratio. But if your down payment is 10 percent—or more— your lender might be comfortable with a monthly housing cost to monthly income ratio that exceeds 28 percent.

Example:

If your gross monthly income equals $5,000, you make a 5 percent cash down payment and your lender uses the 28 percent ratio:

Your maximum monthly payment is $5,000 x .28 = $1,400

Make a 20 percent cash down payment, however, and your lender might feel comfortable using a 33 percent ratio, which would allow you to spend $1,650 on your monthly housing expenses:

Your maximum monthly payment is $5,000 X .33 = $1,650

With this information, you can calculate the purchase price of a home based on your total annual gross income. You also are acquainted with the guidelines most lenders user to determine your maximum monthly expenditure for your mortgage payment, property taxes, insurance and condominium or cooperative fees.

It's time for a quick check:

→ Do you feel you have sufficient income combined with enough money for a down payment to purchase a home?

→ Do you have a steady employment history of two years or more?

If so, congratulations! You've passed the first step toward pre-approval!

If not, there are several things you can do to get there:

→ Look for a co-borrower to increase your gross annual income and ultimately increase your borrowing power

→ Do not buy now, but wait until you:

→ Save more money towards your down payment

→ Find a job making more money (but stay with your current job to avoid a gap in your employment history)

→ Have at least two years employment history

→ Seek alternative financing options (you will learn more about these financing options later)

If you're not qualified now, decide that your renting days will be over—the sooner the better! I'll show you how to do it, but the rest is up to you.

If you're qualified to buy now, do it! DON'T RENT! So let's take a look at what interest rates have to do with qualifying for a mortgage.

Interest Rates/Terms

The majority of your monthly housing expenses pays the mortgage. The amount of your monthly mortgage payment will include principal (the amount you borrowed) and interest (the lender's fee for using the money). Lenders refer to these payments of principal and interest as "P&I."

The lender will use an amortization table to determine the amount of your P&I monthly payment necessary to pay off the loan in the term specified. The amount of the monthly payment is based on several factors:

→ The size of the loan

→ The interest rate

→ The term (or repayment period)

Example:

Example	Mortgage Amount	Interest Rate	Term	Monthly Payment (P & I)
A	$100,000	7.5%	30 Years	$699.21
B	$100,000	7.5%	15 Years	$927.01

at an interest rate of 7.5 percent. This loan has a term of 30 years for repayment. The monthly payment, P&I only, is $699.21, and it's a major component of the monthly housing costs lenders consider for pre-approval.

Example B shows the same loan for a term of 15 years. Notice it has a monthly payment of $927.01; a higher monthly payment is required to pay back $100,000 over a shorter term. The payments in examples A or B, along with all your other housing expenses, can total no more than 28 percent (or more, if applicable) of your gross monthly income.

The amount of interest you are being charged by the lender, as well as the terms of repayment, such as 15 or 30 years, can change your monthly mortgage payment substantially—and have an impact on the lender's qualifying guideline for total monthly housing costs. It is important to select the best mortgage type for your specific situation. You will learn more about mortgage product options in Chapter 9, Obtaining a Loan.

The remaining items lenders consider when pre-approving a buyer are debt and credit history. Are you ready to take another look at where your money is going?

Debt

When lenders are making decisions on how much money to loan to you, they review your existing long-term debt.

Remember, the qualifying guidelines lenders use:

Your monthly housing costs should total no more than 28 percent of your gross monthly income. Your monthly housing costs plus other long-term debts should total no more than 36 percent of your gross monthly income.

If your monthly debt payment is more than allowed for your income level, the amount of money you can borrow for your home purchase will be reduced.

This worksheet will help you calculate your own monthly debt.

Monthly Debt Payment Worksheet

Debt (with 10 or more months payments remaining)	Monthly Payment
Car	$
Average monthly credit card(s)	$
Student loan	$
Medical/health care	$
Alimony/child support	$
Other installment loans (furniture, appliances, etc.)	$
Total Monthly Debt Payments	$

Next, look at the Allowable Monthly Debt Table to see how much existing monthly debt is acceptable for your income level. Compare this figure with your total monthly debt from the previous worksheet.

Well . . . is your total monthly debt payment within the allowable range?

If the answer is yes, GREAT! Again, you passed the test for qualifying. But, if your debt was not within the allowable range, the lender can reduce the amount of money you can borrow. Another "rule of thumb" a lender might use will reduce your total mortgage amount available to you by $5,000 for every $50 of excess allowable debt payment.

Allowable Monthly Debt Table	
Gross Annual Income	Allowable Monthly Debt Payment
$20,000	$133
$25,000	$167
$30,000	$200
$35,000	$233
$40,000	$267
$45,000	$300
$50,000	$333
$55,000	$367
$60,000	$400
$65,000	$432
$70,000	$466
$75,000	$500
$80,000	$533
$85,000	$566
$90,000	$600
$95,000	$633
$100,000	$666

Example:

Your gross annual income =$50,000

Your monthly debt payments = $433

Allowable monthly debt = $333 (from the table)

Subtract your monthly debt from allowable debt as indicated ($433-$333 = $100 of excessive monthly debt)

Divide $100 (excessive monthly debt) by $50 (guideline for excess debt) ($100 divided by $50 = 2)

For every $50 of excess debt, reduce loan by $5,000 ($5,000 x 2 = $10,000)

In this example, your loan amount would be reduced by $10,000 due to excess debt. My suggestion would be to wait. Don't buy now. Increase your borrowing power by paying off some debt before buying a home, or consolidate debts into a lower-interest rate loan.

Credit History

Now that we've examined your debt, let's see what your credit record looks like. The term "credit" means that you are using borrowed money to pay for something you purchased. Lenders like to see some history of your debts and repayment of them. They love good credit! Good credit means that you repay the borrowed money on time as promised.

Lenders will verify your debt and credit history through a credit report. These reports show how much debt you have and if you made payments on time, or if you paid back the loan at all. When you apply for a loan, you give permission for a lender to order your credit report from a credit-reporting agency.

Your Credit Report Can Be Decisive!

Credit reports contain credit scoring. A credit score, which is assigned after an analysis of your credit profile, can range from the low 400s to the upper 800s. As I noted in the preface, you will need a credit score of at least 620; however, it will be to your financial advantage in today's mortgage market to have a credit score of 740 or higher.

These scores help predict:

→ How likely you are to pay back a loan on time

→ What your interest rates will be (the higher the credit score, the lower the interest rate and vice versa)

In today's economic climate, your credit history and your credit report can be decisive. They're two of the most important factors in your becoming a first-time homebuyer. To prevent surprises, get a copy of your credit report before you seek pre-approval from a lender. You are entitled to one free copy of your credit report per year from each of the three major credit reporting agencies. you can obtain a copy of your credit report from other organizations for a usually modest fee in the $10-$20 range. I believe getting your report before you apply is worth the effort. You can learn if anything in the report could keep you from being approved for a loan.

I've included a great deal of vital information for you in the Appendix of this book. The section includes the names, addresses, telephone numbers and websites of the three major agencies, a sample dispute letter and advice about dealing with companies that claim to "repair" your credit. Please refer to it.

Getting your credit report can have three different outcomes. Your credit report will:

→ be favorable, with no problems;

→ be unfavorable, with problems that can take time to resolve;

➜ or it will contain what you believe to be inaccurate, incomplete or unverifiable information.

Let's see what you can and should do in each scenario.

If Your Credit Report Is Favorable

Congratulations! You've completed one critically important step in your journey toward homeownership. Keep up the good work by paying your bills on time, maintaining your credit card debt at the lowest practicable levels and continuing to save for that proverbial "rainy day."

If Your Credit Report Is Unfavorable

If your credit report contains accurate but unfavorable information, *you probably should wait to buy a home. Work on repairing your credit profile instead.* You can do it, but you simply must give it the time and attention it requires. If you have more debt than the allowable amount for your income level, you need a plan to eliminate it. You worked through the Monthly Expense Tracking Worksheet in Chapter 1 and developed a plan to reduce your debt. If you make late debt payments frequently, you may not be considered a good candidate for a loan. You probably will need to show a two-year history of timely payments before you can start to look for a home again.

If you choose to work with a business that promises to help you repair your credit history, proceed slowly.

The Federal Trade Commission has taken a strong position against what it titles "The Scam"—companies that appeal to consumers with poor credit histories. Referring to these organizations, the FTC says: "They promise, for a fee, to clean up your credit report so you can get a car loan, a home mortgage, insurance, or even a job. The truth is, they can't deliver."

I've included the complete text of the FTC advice to consumers in the Appendix. It is available on the internet at http://www.ftc.gov/bcp/conline/pubs/credit/repair.shtm

If Your Credit Report Is Wrong

If you believe your credit report contains inaccurate, incomplete, or unverifiable information, the Fair Credit Reporting Act gives you the right to dispute that information. A sample letter requesting a correction from the appropriate reporting agency is provided in the Appendix. It is essential that you contact the agency which issued the negative report. *If there are unresolved credit problems on the report, your loan agent can tell you what to do to about them.*

More Credit Information is Available

To learn more about credit scores and credit reporting agencies, go to www.annualcreditreport.com.

Non-Traditional Credit History

But what do you do if you don't have any credit history? You don't use credit cards? You never had an auto loan because you saved money from a part-time job and paid cash for your used car? You never had a student loan? Your parents planned for your college education and paid for all of it. Lucky you!

If that's the case, it's time to get creative. You'll have to come up with a credit history some other way. It's called a "nontraditional" credit history.

I have some questions for you:

→ Do you or have you paid rent to a landlord?

→ Do you pay or have you paid for utilities, such as gas, electricity, cable, or telephone?

→ Are you paying for your car insurance or medical insurance on a regular basis?

If you answered yes to some or all of those questions, you can establish a "non-traditional" credit history by providing documentation of these payments. Cancelled checks and printouts from the companies you paid regularly provide proof. You can ask these companies to provide a letter or computer printout showing how long you've been a customer and your payment history. Obtain at least two years of regular payment documentation and show it to the loan agent.

Savings Accounts

In addition to your credit history, the mortgage lender will want proof you saved most if not all the money for the down payment and part or all of the closing costs. You will need your financial institution to verify the amount of money you saved and how long the funds have been in your account.

There may be programs in your community to help first-time buyers with a down payment. You may be able to accept a gift from a relative or get a grant or other available funds you do not have to repay, or borrow some of the money from a local nonprofit organization or government agency. I will review these down payment options in Chapter 9, Obtaining a Mortgage.

If you regularly saved cash in a savings account for the purpose of the down payment and other home buying expenses, congratulations! You will fly through this step of the qualification process, I'm sure.

If you don't have records showing you saved some of the money for the down payment yourself, you should not consider buying a home now.

Revisit your Monthly Expense Tracking Worksheet completed in Chapter 1 and make sure you have a plan to save for a down payment and other costs. Open a savings account and put money into it on a regular basis so a future lender will see you save consistently and are ready to apply for a mortgage.

Let's review where you are now:

→ You know the qualifying guidelines lenders use.

→ You know what your monthly debt payments are and whether you need to eliminate debt or establish a consistent, on-time history of paying your debts.

→ You also understand why credit history is important to lenders and why you must repair bad credit before buying a home.

→ You are aware that you must have proof that you alone saved for some or all of your down payment and other closing costs.

If you feel confident you can get pre-approved, you are ready to see a lender or mortgage broker. I'll provide more information in Chapter 9. If not, you have some work to do to get ready for pre-approval.

What's Next?

Before meeting with a loan agent, make sure you have this information, which is necessary for you to get a pre-approval:

→ Recent paycheck stub

→ Two years of income tax forms if you are self-employed

→ Verification from your bank showing regular deposits towards your down payment

→ Verification of employment showing length of employment (it's helpful if you can get a letter or other document from your employer indicating you will continue to be employed)

You have many opportunities to keep your good credit or to

Pre-Approval Checklist	
Use this checklist as a guide to get ready for pre-approval.	
Obtain and review your Credit Report Do you have good credit? Or . . . do you need to improve it?	
Correct errors on Credit Report, if any	
Make loan payments on time every month	
Take control of your credit Reduce debt Use credit cards wisely Only apply for credit you really need Call your creditors if you need assistance	
Create non traditional credit history if you do not have any loans or credit cards	
Track monthly expenses, create a budget, establish a checking account and a savings account to manage your money	

improve your credit. Some of the suggestions I provided may take a few months to implement; others will take a few years.

Either way, make the commitment to being a homeowner. DON'T RENT . . . You Can Buy! Make the decision to get started now.

Now that you know the requirements for pre-approval, let's find out what kind of home you want to purchase and where you would like to live.

4

What Do You Want In a Home?

Decisions . . . Decisions . . .

By now you have a pretty good idea about how much money you can afford to spend on a home. Perhaps you've scanned the newspaper or surfed the Internet to see what interest rates are available. You know your credit is good and you're confident you can pre-qualify for a loan. With that preliminary work behind you, you're ready to embark on one of the most challenging and rewarding phases of home ownership: shopping.

What do you want? What do you

Home Buying Checklist	✓
Get Pre-Approved	✓
Prepare a Wish List/ Choose a Location	✓
Find an Agent	
Look for a Home	
Negotiate the Purchase	
Hire an Inspector	
Obtain a Mortgage	
Close the Deal	

need? What do you like? What don't you like? Where will you look? It's a challenge to sort through all of these decisions. Buying a home is probably the largest purchase you'll ever make in your lifetime and as you know, it's important to get it right!

Some people intuitively know what they want; others need some help analyzing their needs. This chapter can serve as a guide if you think you need help with your home-buying decisions or as a checklist if you don't.

Do You Know What You're Looking For?

Before you start looking at properties on the market, take the time to think about the kind of features that are important to you and your family. Perhaps you want larger rooms, or more of them. Maybe you are tired of sharing laundry facilities with the neighbors. Or you want your own yard so the children can be supervised easily while they play. Whatever it is, make sure you know what you want *before* you start looking.

Years ago, people bought a home and lived there most of their adult lives. Today, the average length of stay in one home is 5 to 7 years, so I suggest you look at a home that will meet your needs for at least the next 5 years.

> "... look at a home that will meet your needs for at least the next 5 years."

Another consideration is resale. Because you probably won't live for the rest of your life in the first home you buy, evaluate houses with an eye to the future. Ask yourself "How desirable will this house be when I want move?" Will a two-bedroom, one bath single-family house be as desirable to others as a three-bedroom, two bath house? How will a house with five bedrooms, a small kitchen and no dining room appeal to a family with children? Just because you can use extra bedrooms for storage does not make a house a good resale candidate. In this case, you would be better advised to find a a home with a basement or perhaps a large garage to use for storage purposes. But don't get caught up in hypothetical examples. Let's look at some of the many considerations you'll want to take in to account in your search for your first home.

I'd suggest you consider your lifestyle needs, look at older and new construction to decide which you prefer and then decide how much space—inside and out—you want. And while you're shopping, I'd also suggest you look at the array of housing types available to you, from single family detached homes to townhouses to condos and coops.

Lifestyle Features

Consider your lifestyle. Do you entertain a lot? If so, you may want a formal dining room. If not, an eat-in kitchen may accommodate your needs. Do you need a one car or two-car garage? Do you need a garage at all? How about a second bathroom or a whirlpool tub? A wood-burning fireplace? Air-conditioning?

Maybe you have special needs that require wheelchair accessibility or a bedroom with a full bath on the first floor. Do you want a family room on the main level or a finished basement so your teens can socialize with friends far away from your quiet space?

New House or Old?

Some people like to move into brand new homes. Others prefer existing homes. And still many other people like older homes that they can fix up, especially if they are handy.

A house that needs "a little tender loving care" is typically a house that needs work. These homes are usually the best value because the seller may reduce the cost to accommodate the imperfections and sell "as is."

If you can do the work yourself and have the time to remodel, this may be the home for you. Make sure you have extra cash to do the work or ask the seller for a seller credit at closing for the repairs you will have to make. If you cannot do the repair work yourself, beware! It can be costly to hire professionals to remodel a home.

Many older homes may need a roof, a furnace or a water heater —or they may not have air conditioning, a dishwasher or other amenities you want. You may have to hire a contractor to install appliances or make changes in the building to accommodate the improvements you want. On the positive side, older homes may have more character and come with features such as built-in book-cases, arched doorframes, window seats, hardwood floors and high ceilings.

New construction homes are typically grouped together by a builder. In some cases, this grouping of homes is called a subdivision. The homes in a new subdivision are approximately the same size in square footage and the prices are about the same. The cost to maintain them should be less than older homes because they can offer the latest in efficient heating, ventilation and cooling (HVAC) systems and energy-saving construction techniques.

New homes are appealing because they have never been lived in. There is usually no need to remodel, which can be costly. They tend to be more expensive than older homes, especially when upgrades are added. New homes may not include window treatments or land-scaping, so you will need to allot money for these necessities.

Location

If living close to your job, day care facility, or near public transportation is important to you, choose your home accordingly. Perhaps the quality of the local school system is critical, if you have children. Do you prefer to be within walking distance of restaurants and shops? Or is it OK for you to drive several miles to a nearby mall? Do you like urban, suburban, or rural areas?

I suggest selecting the "best" neighborhood you can afford; fully aware of the fact that "best" is subjective, of course. But another "rule of thumb" says that good schools, proximity to shopping and public transportation and the overall condition of homes in the area will help a home hold its value over the long term.

> **"Do you like urban, suburban, or rural areas?"**

If you cannot afford to buy in the neighborhood where you want to live, consider buying on the border of that community. If living in a specific community is essential, consider buying a less expensive home there, such as a condominium or a townhouse.

Size

Before you decide what kind of house you might be interested in, here are a number of questions I suggest reviewing with your family. Your answers, coupled with the checklist at the end of this chapter, can help you decide what kind of house is most suitable.

Consider these questions:

→ How many rooms will you need now or in the near future? Will your family outgrow this house too soon?

→ If you are not planning on having a big family, is this house too big for you?

→ Do you want a lot of land?

→ Is the yard too much for you to take care of?

→ Can you afford a yard maintenance service?

→ Is the yard too small to plant the vegetable garden you've been dreaming of?

Consider your current and future housing needs and look at homes somewhere in the middle.

Take a good look at the floor plan of the house. Do you step into the living room directly from the front door? Does the layout of rooms fit your family's lifestyle? Is the family room part of the kitchen, adjacent to the living room, or away from the primary living areas? Is there a main hallway throughout the house? Are all rooms accessible from this hall? A home that requires walking through one room to get to another room may not be as desirable as one with a more convenient floorplan.

If you are looking at a two-story home, is there a bathroom on each level of the house? Does the kitchen have enough cabinets to accommodate your dishes and cooking utensils? Will your furniture fit into the rooms, or is it too big? Will you need to buy additional furnishings to fill the house or to replace furniture that won't work in the new space? Is there adequate closet space in each room for your clothes and other personal belongings?

Types of Homes

With those questions answered, let's review the many different types of homes on the market: a single family detached house, a condominium, or a townhouse, to name a few. Perhaps you want to live in a specific area that will dictate the style of home available to you. Where you want to live and how much you want to spend on a home will determine what type of homes you can look at.

Single-Family Detached

The most common type of housing in North America is the single-family detached home—regardless of its size. Its key distinguishing factors are:

→ it sits on its own land (which is sold with the house) and

→ it is not attached to any other residential property.

It's your house—some say your castle—and you can do with it as you wish, within the constraints of city, village or subdivision regulations and ordinances. You can paint it, expand it, landscape it —whatever you want, as long as your changes conform to local code, if applicable.

And because you own the land the house sits on, you will probably have a yard—from a few square feet to acres and acres, it's all yours.

If you like space, aren't bothered by such mandatory chores as mowing the lawn, raking leaves, and, in colder climates, shoveling snow, a single family detached home belongs at the top of your house-hunting list.

You gain a number of advantages: Historically, resale value is the highest on single family detached homes. If you want more room as your family grows or your family's needs change, you can add a room or remodel, subject to code restrictions. Usually, you won't pay property management fees as you would with a townhouse or condominium.

But there are disadvantages to owning a single family detached home: You are totally and completely responsible for all maintenance, repair, landscaping and lawn upkeep. Usually, and in most areas, single family detached homes are more expensive than townhouses or condominiums.

Condominium

Many first time homebuyers choose to purchase a condominium, or condo for short, because the unit is usually smaller and less expensive than single-family housing. Living in a condominium is akin to living in an apartment, but each unit is individually owned.

The common area of the condominium and the space that surrounds the units, including the hallways and elevators, are jointly owned. A monthly fee, called a "condo fee," is charged to individual condominium unit owners to pay for management of the condominium complex, maintenance of the common areas, and in some cases for utility bills. Note that condo fees are not included in the monthly mortgage payment. You will have one more expense, in addition to your mortgage payment, taxes and insurance, when you buy a condo. Condo associations also can make special assessments to pay for extraordinary expenses, such as replacing the building's central heating system or making repairs to the heating, ventilation and air conditioning system.

Townhouse

A townhouse is another type of multiple unit condominium housing. Typically, each townhouse has two or more stories and shares a common wall with an adjacent unit. Each townhouse usually has its own outside patio or yard space, but the ground and other facilities are jointly owned—as are a condominium's. You will be charged dues to pay for the maintenance of the grounds and facilities and other necessary scheduled repairs.

Condos and townhouse complexes usually have a Home Owner's Association with responsibility for enforcing the appropriate covenants, conditions and restrictions (CC&Rs). Read the Association's by-laws because there may be important restrictions on your ability to rent, remodel, and resell the unit you own.

Co-op

Cooperatives, or Co-ops, are similar to condominiums; multiple residents own them, but the residents own shares in the corporation that owns the property. Each resident has the right to occupy a specific apartment or unit.

If a unit occupied by a specific resident is smaller than another resident's unit, that resident will own fewer shares of stock than the other. The more shares of stock owned by a resident, the more power he or she has when an issue regarding the co-op arises.

Cooperative shareholders pay a monthly maintenance fee, a portion of which pays for property taxes and insurance. The co-op's Board of Directors has power of attorney to approve or disapprove any buyer, so it's important that you get acquainted with your possible fellow shareowners. You should also know that lenders consider co-ops the least desirable type of housing to finance.

Duplex

Duplex housing consists of two individual two-story houses joined by one common wall. Most often, each unit-owner individually owns the residential property.

A street built with duplex homes may or may not have a Homeowner's Association. On one hand, having no association fee to pay each month could be a positive; however, you will be responsible for all your home maintenance and repair costs.

". . . guidelines ensure uniformity and are meant to help maintain or increase the value of the homes."

Not having a Homeowner's Association could mean the builder did not or has not established guidelines for future maintenance. Don't forget your home is attached to another. If you need a new roof and your neighbor cannot afford to replace the adjoining roof, what do you do? What might happen if you might paint your duplex blue but your adjoining neighbor paints his unit yellow. Without written rules, how can you prevent or resolve such issues?

Some homebuilders file specific guidelines with the city or village even if there is no Homeowner's Association established. These guidelines ensure uniformity and are meant to help maintain or increase the value of the homes. If you are looking at a duplex home with no Homeowner's Association, seek legal advice to see if there are established maintenance guidelines.

Style, Construction Material, and More

In addition to learning about different types of homes on the market, you will have to think about what style of home you like best. Do you prefer a one story ranch? A split-level? A two-story home with the bedrooms tucked away on the second floor? A Georgian? A Colonial? Cape Cod? Contemporary? Victorian? Your real estate agent can show you homes that match the names.

How about construction materials? Do you want your house to be built of brick? Do you want it to have aluminum or vinyl siding? Is there anything about stucco that you like or dislike? What's popular in the area where you would like to live?

I like to think that shopping for your first home can be enjoyable and educational. The opportunity to own your home is one of this country's greatest gifts and your choices are almost limitless! Your agent can help you pare that vast array of choices to a manageable number, once you've decided you want to own by heeding my advice: Don't Rent!

Develop a Wish List

Whether it's new or old, a townhouse, condo, duplex, co-op, or single-family detached, choose features that best fit your lifestyle and consider the location options available to you.

Complete the "Wish List" on the following pages to help you decide what you would like to have in a house versus what you "must" have when you start to shop for a home.

This Wish List is a great tool to take with you to your real estate agent. Your agent can use the list to find houses for you to view that meet your specifications. The next chapter will tell you how to find an agent and what services to expect.

New Home Wish List

Type of Home:

❏ Existing ❏ New ❏ Old ❏ Single Family

❏ Townhouse ❏ Condo ❏ Duplex ❏ Co-op

❏ Ranch ❏ Two-story ❏ Split-level

❏ Traditional ❏ Contemporary ❏ Other

Construction: ❏ Brick ❏ Alum. Siding

❏ Wood ❏ Stone ❏ Vinyl Siding ❏ Stucco

❏ Cedar Shingles ❏ Cedar Siding ❏ Cement

Lot Size: ❏ Large ❏ Medium ❏ Small

Children in Home:

❏ Male: ❏ Female: ❏ Teens:

Adults in Home:

Room Type & # Wanted: ❏ Bedrooms ❏ Bathrooms

❏ Dining ❏ Family Room ❏ 1st Floor Laundry

❏ 2nd Floor Laundry ❏ Other

Extras: ❏ Fireplace ❏ Garage ❏ Basement

❏ A/C ❏ Porch ❏ Deck ❏ Patio

❏ Whirlpool Bath ❏ Dishwasher ❏ Washer/Dryer ❏ Stove

❏ Refrigerator ❏ Fenced Yard ❏ Other

Special Requirements: ❏ Elevator ❏ Wheel Chair Accessible

❏ 1st floor Bedroom/Bath ❏ Other

Desired Neighborhood: _____

Transportation Requirements: _____

School Requirements: _____

Shopping District Location: _____

Recreational Facilities & Location
(Health Club, Pool): _____

Religious Institutions: _____

Price Range: $_____ to $_____

Cash Down: $_____

Notes:_____

_____

_____

_____

_____

_____

_____

_____

_____

_____

How to Find an Agent

I need a Real Estate Professional!

Choosing the best real estate agent is an important decision for you now. This chapter will help you select the best agent for the scope of professional services you need.

You can buy a home without involving a real estate agent. If you want the purchase of your first home to go smoothly, however, I believe getting the guidance of an expert is your best bet.

You can ask a friend who recently purchased a home for a referral. You'll want to know how responsive the agent

Home Buying Checklist	✓
Get Pre-Approved	✓
Prepare a Wish List/ Choose a Location	✓
Find an Agent	✓
Look for a Home	
Negotiate the Purchase	
Hire an Inspector	
Obtain a Mortgage	
Close the Deal	

was, if phone calls were answered promptly, and if scheduled appointments were kept.

You can meet agents by visiting open houses. Each will be hosted by a real estate professional who is representing a seller. If you're comfortable with the agent's sales approach, you could tell the agent you're going to be house hunting soon. If you like the agent's response, consider working with him or her. You want an agent who will listen closely to you, who will screen properties for you and who can help you negotiate everything from the purchase price to details necessary to close on time.

If the first two options don't work, look at the real estate ads in your local newspaper. Contact any of the agencies listed and ask to have an agent contact you because you're a prospective home buyer.

You can use the Internet, too. Go to the website of a community you're interested in; the chamber of commerce can provide the names of member real estate firms you can contact. Or, if you're in that community, walk into a real estate office you find attractive and ask to be introduced to an agent.

Experience Counts

House hunting can be time consuming. Your time is valuable. With that in mind, look for an experienced agent who specializes in the area where you would like to live; in the kind of house you think you'd like to buy; or in the appropriate price range. You'll gain an immediate advantage—the agent probably has toured or visited most of the houses that meet your price or location criteria.

Many times listing agents—real estate professionals who contract with sellers to market their homes—conduct a sales agent walk-through when a home goes on the market. This gives local real estate agents an opportunity to view the home and helps to sell it. Many agents take advantage of this previewing opportunity to see if the house meets a given client's specifications.

The more homes your agent has viewed in the area you wish to live, the better qualified he or she is to suggest homes for you to see that meet your requirements.

Qualities of a Good Agent

Your agent is your best resource to assist you on your home buying quest . . . IF your Wish List is in the agent's hand; the agent has access to a computerized multiple listing service (MLS), an automated system for generating lists of houses that match your specific requirements; and first hand knowledge of the homes in a specific area.

In addition to house hunting, your agent should be able to refer related professional services to you, such as lenders, attorneys, home inspectors and insurance companies. A good agent will be right there with you need these services. He or she should help make your home buying experience as pleasant, efficient and pro-ductive as possible.

It's important to choose your real estate professional wisely because you will be spending a lot of time together until you find the house you want to buy. You might want to conduct interviews with several agents.

Evaluate each person you talk with according to these suggested questions:

→ Is the agent friendly?

→ Is the agent licensed?

→ Does the agent work full time in real estate?

→ Does the agent have access to the MLS?

→ Is the agent a clear communicator?

→ Is the agent a good listener?

→ Do your questions get answered?

→ Do you feel like you can trust this agent?

→ Is the agent knowledgeable about various neighborhoods, especially the one you wish to live in and areas surrounding it?

→ Does this agent seem organized?

→ Will you receive listing sheets prior to viewing homes?

→ Can this agent refer other professional services to you, if you buy?

→ What types of organizations does the agent belong to in the community?

→ Does the agent seem honest and fair?

→ Are your phone calls returned promptly?

Now that you have some information that will help you evaluate the agents before selecting your agent, let's see how they get paid for their services and what the terms agent, broker, salespeople, and REALTOR®mean.

Who Pays Your Agent?

In most residential real estate transactions, two real estate professionals will be involved—one working with you and the other working with the seller. A predetermined percentage of the commission is divided between these professionals. Technically, therefore, both agents work for the seller.

Remember that when you negotiate the price of a home you want to purchase. The agent you have been working with is obligated to look out for the *seller's* best interests. After all, it's the seller who is paying the commission earned by both agents, if two agents are involved in the transaction.

That has changed in the last few years. In some states, buyers hire agents to represent them, which means these agents work for and are paid by the buyer.

However, traditional methods of commission payment remain popular in most areas across the United States. As a first time homebuyer, it's a good idea to ask your agent who pays for his or her services.

Let's get familiar with the different levels of service real estate agents provide.

Types of Agents

Real estate professionals who sell homes must be licensed by the state in which they work. These professionals are known as agents, brokers, salespersons, or REALTORs®. Most people use these terms generically, but they have distinctive differences professionally. It's a good idea to know the qualifications of the person who will be working with you.

Broker/Salesperson

Brokers and salespeople can represent either the seller or buyer in real estate transactions. But a broker's license requires that the broker have more professional education than a real estate salesperson. Part of this higher level of certification qualifies a broker to open and maintain a real estate office, if desired.

Brokers who work under the supervision of another broker are called associate brokers. They can work independently, without supervision. A salesperson, in contrast, always must work under a broker's supervision.

Agents

Brokers and salespeople can be called agents. A broker's title will depend on the role being executed at the time of the sale. If a broker is working for another broker and sells a home, he or she is considered the agent for that sale. Salespeople, on the other hand, are always agents.

Realtor

A REALTOR®is an agent who holds a membership to the National Association of Realtors (NAR). Not all agents are Realtors.

Part/Full Time Agents

Many licensed real estate agents work part-time. Some have full time jobs; some are retired and do not want to work too many hours; others choose to represent one client at a time for various reasons. Even though part-time agents are qualified and licensed to sell homes, they may not be as familiar with the current market as full-time agents.

The choice between a full- or a part-time agent is yours, of course. I would encourage you to select an agent you trust, who will be available to you on your schedule and who is actively involved in the local real estate community.

Commit to your Agent

When you select an agent, make the commitment to work with that agent. To a real estate agent, time is money—and if you waste their time working with several agents, don't be surprised if all of them are reluctant to be of much assistance to you.

> **"When you select an agent, make the commitment to work with that agent."**

If you're looking in several geographically distinct communities, it's possible to work with more than one agent. In this case,

I'd suggest you tell each agent what you're doing, and why. If that's a problem, discuss it before it becomes an impediment to your working relationship. But be a loyal buyer and commit the sale to the agent who shows you the home you choose to buy. That agent is entitled to the commission.

If you see an open house and stop to view it, make sure you mention you're working with an agent. It is important to let the hosting agent know he or she will not represent you. Direct some of the questions you may have about the property to your own agent for follow up.

> "... be a loyal buyer and commit the sale to the agent who shows you the home you choose to buy."

If you're not satisfied with the agent you're working with, you can terminate the relationship if you have not entered into a contract to buy a home.

If you decide you are not satisfied and you've entered into a contract to purchase a home, it's difficult to change agents. Rather than terminate your working relationship, I suggest you tell the agent of your concerns as soon as they develop. If the conversation you have with your agent isn't satisfactory, contact the agent's supervisor and ask to have someone else from the office finish the transaction. You can also ask an attorney to monitor the transaction.

Now that you see how painless first time home buying can be if you select a real estate agent who is a good listener, communicates clearly, is knowledgeable about the community and shows you homes that meet your requirements, to name a few good qualities . . . DON'T RENT!!!

Get out there *now* and start looking for an agent to show you homes.

The next chapter will provide information on where to find homes for sale and will give you some tools to track and compare your findings.

6

Looking For a Home

Expect to Make Compromises

It's exciting to realize you don't have to rent ever again! But finding the best home for you and your family is no small task. Your wish list helped you focus on the features you want in a home. The more homes you look at with those features included, the easier it will be for you to choose the right one to buy. A good location is essential, of course. It's important to consider which neighborhood appeals to you, whether you like the schools in the area, if shopping is near by, and other essential factors. As you know, you have many types of

Action	✓
Get Pre-Approved	✓
Prepare a Wish List/ Choose a Location	✓
Find an Agent	✓
Look for a Home	✓
Negotiate the Purchase	
Hire an Inspector	
Obtain a Mortgage	
Close the Deal	

homes to choose from, including condominiums, townhouses, new homes or older ones.

In this chapter, you will learn where to find information about homes for sale. I'll introduce you to a homebuyer's checklist to help you keep records of the homes you view to make better buying decisions. And finally, you will learn how to look for a home that provides gift money to people who qualify for a loan. These programs make it easier to buy, so DON'T RENT!

Most homebuyers have to decide which features outweigh others in their final decision to buy a home. Compromise can be expected unless a home is custom built to your specifications.

For example: You might want an older home because you believe older homes have more character than newer homes. But you discover that older homes in the neighborhood you like have detached garages that face the alley at the back of the house. You prefer an attached garage because it's much more convenient in bad weather and it shortens trips from the car to the kitchen when you've been grocery shopping. You can choose to stick with your initial intentions—find an older house—or you can compromise. The choice is yours.

> **"Compromise can be expected unless a home is custom built to your specifications."**

In this example, you might decide to look at homes new enough to have attached garages. But what if there aren't any newer homes in this area? You might consider moving to the outskirts of the community to get the home that's best for you and your family.

You may have to compromise on location, the size of the home, brick construction or aluminum siding, the number of bathrooms you want, or something else. You can hire a carpenter to add some of that character you are looking for, such as built in bookcases. These adjustments to your original "wish list" are not that difficult to make once you begin to compare homes. To do that, you need to know how to find homes that are on the market.

Locating Homes For Sale

Some people like to rely solely on their real estate agent to locate homes for them to see. Others like to participate in the search for the right house. The more homes you view, the better you will be at making the right decisions. There are several ways to identify homes that are on the market:

→ Classified Ads (Internet, Newspapers, Shopper's Guides)

→ Word of mouth

→ For Sale Signs

Classified Ads

If you want to find classified ads with leads to "Open House" listings, you can begin by searching the real estate section of your local newspaper or by looking through shopper's guides, which are small real estate magazines published by local real estate companies. You can find your local newspaper or shopper's guide on the Internet, at a newsstand, at your grocery store, pharmacy, or at a variety of stores.

The Internet provides information about buying real estate from many sources. You can look under specific real estate brokerage company sites, Multiple Listing Services (MLS), the local newspaper and for virtually any city's shopper's guides and other publications.

If you're starting your research on homes for sale, type "homes for sale" and the name of the community you're interested in into your favorite search engine to generate a list of sites that contain information about that market. From there, you can easily view listings of homes and learn a lot about the city as well. You can do this for almost any city, town or community you're interested in.

You can call your agent, the local Association of Realtors, or a local real estate company to learn how to access local real estate listings on-line. If you contact a real estate company for information but have an agent, make sure you mention that fact. If you don't have an agent to work with, this is another opportunity to meet prospective agents.

Word of Mouth

Another great way to learn about homes for sale or homes that will be put on the market soon is by word of mouth. All you have to do is tell your friends you're house hunting, what your needs are, and where you want to live. You'll be surprised to learn how many people know someone who is selling a home. And you might get lucky and hear about a home before it goes on the market.

A friend of mine heard about a home that had gone on the market a few hours before, but had not been keyed into the MLS system. My friend was able to negotiate a better price for the home because the broker was willing to forego some of the commission. The broker spent nothing on marketing the home and was willing to accept a lower commission in return for a quick sale.

If you want to buy a house that's not yet on the market, the seller might be willing to negotiate a better sale price in return for a quicker sale. Many sellers will take advantage of a quick sale to avoid the time and effort required for showings, open houses and other intrusions into the lives and schedules of their families. Everything is negotiable. All you have to do is ask!

For Sale Signs

When you decide on a neighborhood you like, drive or walk around in search of "For Sale" signs. This is a great way to find houses being sold by owner (called "fizzbows" by the pros—a "For Sale by Owner" acronym).

Pay attention to these signals while driving or walking in different neighborhoods:

→ **Do most of the homes appear to be well maintained?** Well-maintained homes fortify the value of the neighborhood and its homes. It says the homeowners value their property and take care of their investments. This is important when you want to sell your home.

→ **Is there a consistent style or look to the neighborhood's houses?** Avoid buying a home that has a dramatically different style than the other homes on the block (such as a contemporary ranch house on a block with all Victorian homes). The value of that home could be lower because it does not fit into the character of the neighborhood.

→ **Are there signs of community activity?** Are there any children on playgrounds, people walking or biking? Do you see any bike or walking paths? If these activities are important to you, do you see people doing the things you like to do? Are facilities nearby for activities you and your family enjoy?

→ **Do you see signs of children?** Look for clues that children live nearby—houses with swing sets, toys or bikes in their yards.

→ **Are there any religious, educational, or recreational facilities in the area?** If proximity to such facilities is important to you, I suggest you determine their locations, how to get there and how long the trip will take when you're most likely to go there. If public schools are a factor, make sure the home is within the boundaries of the school district you prefer.

→ **Are there a large number of homes on the market in the immediate area? If so, why?** Investigate why people are moving. Are taxes being raised to pay for additional educational facilities? Are residents relocating because an air traffic

pattern creates high noise levels or a street or nearby express-
way is being enlarged to accommodate more traffic?. Are
there plans to change the zoning regulations? If so, find out
how that will affect the neighborhood.

→ **Is shopping or public transportation nearby?** If you don't
have a car, you will want to see if shopping and public transportation are within walking distance.

→ **Is this a good location?** Is the home located on a busy street?
Is there a shopping center right behind the house? Are there
train tracks one block over?

New Construction

If you've looked at homes under construction or new and unoc-
cupied homes, I want to provide some additional guidance for your
consideration.

First, deal with a reputable builder. You can get information
about builders from the National Association of Home Builders at
www.NAHB.org.

Second, you can use the gap between making an offer on a home
under construction and the completion date to add to your savings
for the down payment or to pay down existing long-term debt.

Third, you can use the gap between your offer and completion
to make a number of choices about the house while it's under construction. You might have the opportunity to select cabinetry,
flooring and appliances, for example.

Fourth, if you decide to make a down payment on a home under
construction, write your deposit check to a title company, rather
than the builder. This protects you in case the builder encounters
unforeseen financial problems or for some reason is unable to complete the construction of the home you want to buy.

Once you have looked at the homes you wanted to see, you're
ready to compare their features, strengths and potential weaknesses.

It's easy to forget some important details if you toured 10 to 15 homes over a period of time. The details are essential for you to make good home buying decisions, so use the system I suggest for keeping track of each house you visit. This will help you stay organized and you won't forget or confuse important details.

Record Keeping

Some features important to you might not be included on the MLS printout provided by the real estate agent. As a supplement, use the House Evaluation Checklist below and a digital camera to compare house features and prices.

Home Buyer's Checklist

Location: _____   Sq. Ft. _____

Price: _____   Neighborhood: _____

# of Bedrooms: _____   # of Bathrooms: _____

EXTERIOR

Condition:	❏ Good	❏ Fair	❏ Poor
Roof:	❏ Good	❏ Fair	❏ Poor
Landscaping:	❏ Patio	❏ Deck	❏ Pool
	❏ Hot Tub	❏ Sprinkler	❏ Play Area

INTERIOR

Living Room:	❏ Fireplace	Colors:	
	Carpet:	Walls:	
Family Room:	Colors:	Carpet:	Walls:
Kitchen:	❏ Eat-in	Floor Type:	
❏ Refrigerator	❏ Disposal	❏ Dish Washer	❏ Microwave
❏ Range	❏ Gas	❏ Electric	❏ Fans/hood
❏ Compactor	Cabinets:	Counter Tops:	

Dining Room:	Colors:	Flooring:	
Master Suite:	Walls:	Colors:	Carpet:
Features:			
Master Bath:	Walls:	Colors:	Flooring:
❑ Soaking Tub	❑ Whirlpool Tub	❑ Shower	# of Sinks
Bedroom 2:	Walls:	Colors:	Flooring:
Bedroom 3:	Walls:	Colors:	Flooring:
Bedroom 4:	Walls:	Colors:	Flooring:
Miscellaneous:	❑ Furnace	Type/Age	❑ A/C
	❑ Pest Report		

Closets/Storage: _____

Garage   ❑ Attached   ❑ Detached   # of Cars:

Schools: _____

Transportation: _____

Stores: _____

Taxes: _____

Summary

I like: _____

I don't like: _____

The house needs: _____

Score: 1 2 3 4 5

Remarks: _____

_____

_____

_____

_____

Gift Programs

DON'T RENT when you have opportunity to buy! There are many state and local government programs offering gift money for down payments on a home. These gifts can help buyers who lack the resources to qualify for a loan but otherwise meet the criteria.

Some gift programs are offered by builders or sellers; others might be available through state or local housing agencies.

If you find a home you would like to buy but you don't have the necessary financial resources or qualifications, check with the local housing authority to see if a gift program is available. You will learn more about available gift programs in the chapter on obtaining a loan.

You now know how to find classified ads containing homes for sale, you have a tool to help you jog your memory on features of homes you view, and you know you DON'T have to RENT even if you are short on cash.

Let's keep going. I want to help you learn how to negotiate with the seller when you are ready to purchase your first home!

7

CHAPTER

Negotiating the Purchase

Decision Making Factors

When you find a home you like, and after comparing its features to those of all the other homes you viewed, and it's your favorite, it's time to make an offer. And it's time to find out how to negotiate the purchase.

In this chapter you will learn several key factors to consider when deciding how much to offer for the home you want. You will also get acquainted with the intricacies of making an offer and a counteroffer.

Action	✓
Get Pre-Approved	✓
Prepare a Wish List/ Choose a Location	✓
Find an Agent	✓
Look for a Home	✓
Negotiate the Purchase	✓
Hire an Inspector	
Obtain a Mortgage	
Close the Deal	

73

Considerations

Some buyers get their adrenalin going just thinking about negotiating. They love to barter! Other buyers are uncomfortable at this stage and worry that something might go wrong.

I encourage you to think of negotiating as just another step in the home buying process. Ultimately, you and the seller will agree on the details of the sale or you will go back one step and begin the process anew.

The amount to consider offering for a home depends on the dynamics of these factors:

→ Local Market Value

→ Condition of the Property

→ Seller's Circumstances

→ Price you can Afford

→ Seller's Contribution (if any)

It's important to consider each factor before you begin to negotiate, so let's look at them individually.

Local Market Value

The economic concept of "supply and demand" applies to residential real estate, too. When a limited number of similar homes are on the market and many buyers want them, the selling price will be higher. Conversely, when there are many homes on the market and few buyers, the selling price will be lower. The listing price does not determine market value or selling price.

Market value is "the theoretical highest price a buyer, willing but not compelled to buy, would pay, and the lowest price a seller, willing but not compelled to sell, would accept."[1] Unfortunately we don't always know the circumstances surrounding a sale. For instance, if repairs are required, the seller may give credit to a buyer, which can make the selling price appear higher.

Here's an example:

The sale price of a home is $185,000. But the buyer negotiated a credit of $5000 to upgrade the landscaping and another $5000 to replace the carpet throughout the home (this credit is called the Seller's Contribution). The buyer paid $175,000 for the home, but the market price, or sale price, was $185,000.

$185,000	Sale Price of the Home
- $5,000	Credit for Landscaping
- $5,000	Credit for Carpet
$175,000	Actual Amount Paid for the Home

It's also possible for a buyer to negotiate a selling price lower than the listing price. Using the example I just related, the "local market value" of the same house, sold but negotiated differently, would be $175,000.00.

Because sellers usually list their homes at a price higher than they expect to receive, it's important to be prepared with as much information as you can before you begin to negotiate.

Ask your agent for a comparative market analysis (CMA), a report containing information about the recent sale of similar homes in the area. This report shows the list prices of comparable homes (called comps) currently on the market or under contract, and the selling price of homes that have closed in the past several months.

"Comparable" means the homes are as similar as possible to the home you are considering—the same number of bedrooms and baths, similar construction, about the same age, and on a lot of the same or near-same size are key comparisons. Comps that date back a year or more might suggest the neighborhood is very stable—a good sign. However, if the market has changed dramatically over the last year—in either direction—don't rely on older comps to provide authoritative guidelines to your initial offer.

You might want to drive past these homes and compare their curb appeal to the home you are considering. Curb appeal is the favorable (or unfavorable) impression the property makes on you as you view it from the street. Houses with positive curb appeal are more attractive to potential buyers because they have more perceived value than homes with little or no curb appeal.

When considering how to value the seller's remodeling or renovation projects, realize that remodeling or adding something to a property does not necessarily add value. In some climates, an in-ground or above-ground swimming pool can detract from a home's value, due to the maintenance costs required to keep either in working order.

Remodeled kitchens and bathrooms reap the highest return on investment to the seller. Additions to a home, such as a family room or a second bathroom, are good investments for the seller and the buyer.

How much to pay for renovations depends on the quality of the work and the materials used—and on the value you place on the improvement and its functionality.

Condition of the Property

Look at the home for potential structural problems and ask your agent and the owner about the condition of the home's heating, plumbing, air conditioning and electrical systems.

It's the responsibility of the real estate agent and the seller to disclose any defects in the house. Both can be held liable by failing to disclose known defects. You will learn more about "disclosures" in the next chapter.

You might also want to ask if the seller plans on completing any repair or remedial work as part of the sale agreement. Sometimes you can get the property at a lower price if the seller does not have to make repairs before the sale.

When preparing your proposed sales contract for an existing

house, include the right to have a professional home inspection conducted as one of your contingencies. You will learn more about " home inspections" in the next chapter. The condition of the property will affect how much you should offer for it.

Seller's Circumstances

It's important to find out as much information as possible about why the property is on the market, and for how long. Consider asking your agent the following questions:

→ Is the seller anxious to move?

→ Is there a job transfer involved?

→ Is there a divorce pending?

→ Does the seller have a contract on another house dependent on the sale of this one?

Answers to these questions can influence your negotiating power.

When you learn how long the house has been on the market, ask if the initial listing price has been lowered. If so, find out when. If the price was reduced within the past few weeks, you probably won't see another reduction soon.

Also ask how frequently the property is being shown. The fewer the showings, especially recent showings, the less buyer interest in the property. If you're interested, and if you have information about the seller's circumstances, you might be able to make a more favorable offer.

You will want to know if the seller has received any offers. If so, instruct your agent to ask what was the highest offer the seller refused. If possible, inquire about the price the seller paid for the house and when it was purchased. This may help you determine how the listing price was calculated, based on inflation over time and the value of the improvements made to the house by the seller.

All of these facts can help you make an informed decision about your offer. Do your homework! You don't want to pay too much for a home or lose the deal if your offer is too low.

Price You Can Afford

Because you've pre-qualified for a mortgage, you know how much money you can spend each month. Remember the term PITI (principle, interest, taxes, and insurance) from Chapter 3? In order to calculate the PITI for a specific house, and to know if you can afford it, you'll need to get the annual cost of:

→ Property taxes

→ Homeowner's insurance

→ Current interest rate (for the mortgage programs you are considering)

→ Association fee (if applicable)

Some MLS listings will provide this information.

It's a good idea to obtain a month-by-month accounting of all utility expenses. This provides you with additional information about your anticipated monthly expenses. It also could highlight extraordinary utility costs that might indicate a problem with insulation or an energy-inefficient HVAC system.

In addition to these projected monthly expenses, you'll need enough money to cover your down payment and closing costs. Make sure your offer falls within your prequalification guidelines.

Seller's Contribution

Here are some negotiating points you don't want to overlook, because they might help you reduce the sale price considerably. You may be willing to accept the price of the home if the seller is willing to incur some of the fees typically paid by the buyer, such as the home inspection, title search, or other settlement costs.

The seller can contribute up to 6% of the sale price of the house; it's called the "seller's contribution." In some cases, the seller and the buyer can split certain fees.

For example:

If . . .	Then . . .
You think the house is priced too high and needs too much work after you reviewed the comparative market analysis (CMA) and looked at the homes that sold in the area in the last few months ...	Use the CMA report and photos of homes sold at those prices to negotiate a lower price based on the money you will need to spend to bring the home up to the local market value.
The seller put a third full bathroom in a two-bedroom house and increased the selling price to cover the total expense of adding the bathroom ...	Negotiate less than the total cost of the bathroom because a two-bedroom house typically does not warrant three full baths.
The house is 27 years old and still has its original roof which shows evidence of age ...	Ask the seller for a roof allowance to cover the cost of replacement.

Strategize your Negotiation

Let's review a possible approach to your first negotiation.

Property Address:

_____

_____

_____

What upgrades did the seller make to the property (if any)?

What is the list price?

Is this price reduced? If so, when?

What was the original list price?

What is the local market value? (see CMA Report)

How long has this property been on the market?

Has there been any past offers? If so, why didn't it sell?

Local Market Conditions

What is the average time to sell? (see CMA Report)

What is the average sale price?

How many similar properties are on the market now?

Have there been any recent improvements to any of these homes?

Condition of the Property

Curb appeal? ❏ Excellent ❏ Good ❏ Average ❏ Poor

Any defects to the house reported by seller/agent?

Any visual property defects?

Any structural problems?

Any major systems need work? (heat, electric, plumbing, A/C)

Original roof, furnace, A/C?

If not, when were they replaced?

Cost of required work?

Will seller contribute?

Seller's Circumstances

Reason for sale?

Did seller purchase another home?

When does seller want to close?

How often is the house being shown?

Is the selling price flexible?

What did the seller pay for the house, and when?

Price you can Afford

Total utility costs per month?

How much are the taxes?

How much is the association fee (if any)?

What is the cost of the homeowner's insurance?

What interest rate will you be paying?

How much is your down payment?

Seller Contribution

Is the seller willing to contribute to any of the closing fees?

Is the seller giving you any allowances? (landscaping, carpet, appliances, for example)

If so, how much?

What percentage of the sale does that equate to? (up to 6%)

Is this Property Affordable?

Can I afford the full asking price?

Are all appliances included in the sale?

Which appliances/fixtures are excluded?

Total amount of seller's contribution?

Key Negotiation Points:

_____

_____

_____

_____

_____

_____

Here's a scenario based on my own experience in working with first time buyers.

The house you wish to buy is a little more than you can afford. There are extensive upgrades in the home because the seller had no intentions of leaving. The seller is very talented and did all of his own remodeling. He purchased top of the line products and material because he works for a builder's supply company and bought almost everything at wholesale.

> **"Here's a scenario based on my own experience in working with first time buyers."**

The property has been on the market for four months and the seller is anxious to move. The list price on the house was lowered one month ago, but the seller is yet to get an offer. Several similar houses are for sale in the neighborhood; their list prices are considerably less. Most of the houses have been remodeled, but their improvements pale in comparison to your seller's house.

The seller, who has accepted a new job in another state, starts in four weeks. He bought a house there and closes on it in two weeks.

Based on this information, you can develop your negotiating strategy knowing that:

→ The home is priced higher than similar homes for sale in the neighborhood (Back up that information with the CMA report)

→ The list price was lowered once and no offers were presented on the home. Perhaps the seller is considering another price reduction.

→ You might be willing to absorb a percentage of the costs of the upgrades, but not all costs. (You might be willing to pay as much as the highest priced similar home in the neighborhood sold for . . . See CMA report.)

→ You don't want to pay for remodeling, including the extensive upgrades using such top of the line products as granite counter tops, designer faucets and imported ceramic tile, because they do not offer a return on your investment.

→ The seller remodeled the home himself, saving labor costs.

→ The seller paid wholesale prices on products and supplies for remodeling.

→ The seller is anxious to sell before closing on new home in two weeks.

→ The seller wants to move before starting his new job in four weeks.

→ No one wants to pay for two mortgages!

Negotiating the Purchase Offer

With this preliminary information in hand, feel confident about getting the negotiation process underway. Your agent is the best person to negotiate the terms. Remind yourself that the agent typically acts on behalf of the seller; keep your emotions out of the negotiation process. Before you begin, decide on the maximum price you are willing to pay for the home and stick to it!

This is a critical point in the purchase process, and I suggest you follow my advice closely:

→ Negotiate in writing only. Verbal negotiations and agreements don't carry the force of a written contract.

→ Be assertive. Challenge anything that makes you uncomfortable. Be prepared to negotiate, based on the decision-making facts you have at hand.

→ Offer less than you are prepared to pay because sellers ask for more than they expect to receive.

→ Obtain a pre-approval letter from your lender. This ensures a lender's financing commitment.

→ Expect to submit deposit or earnest money with your offer.

→ Be willing to walk away if the negotiations are not satisfactory. Other opportunities await you.

Don't worry! Negotiating the purchase of a house consists of an offer and, usually, a series of counteroffers. Good faith bargaining on both sides usually moves you closer to making a deal, rather than further away.

Let's find out how to price your initial offer.

Pricing the Offer

Starting your offer at about 10% under the asking price is another "rule of thumb" for homes fairly priced in average to slow local market conditions. But be careful not to insult the seller with an offer that's far below the list price. You run the risk of presenting yourself as an opportunistic, "bottom-fishing" buyer who isn't interested in the property or in meaningful negotiations. A lower than usual offer might be appropriate, and considered by the seller, if you're confident the seller wants a quick transaction. Perhaps you know about a pending divorce or another situation that would make the seller more anxious to sell than usual.

If the property is overpriced or needs a lot of work, consider presenting a low offer. After you've done your homework on similar homes that sold in the area (properties identified in your CMA or comp report) and if you feel confident the house you want is overpriced, start with a lower offer. This gives you the advantage of significantly more bargaining power. You can seek allowances on repairs or other seller contributions.

> **". . . be careful not to insult the seller with an offer that's far below the list price."**

If it's a seller's market, meaning the market is "hot," a well-priced home can sell at its asking price— or above. If you start your offer in a seller's market at about 5% below asking price, the seller will know you are a serious buyer. If you've decided where to price your offer, then . . . DON'T RENT!!! It's time to buy.

Submitting the Offer

Once you decide how much you are willing to pay for a house, which factors you will use to negotiate, and how to price the initial offer, you are ready to ask your agent to submit the offer in writing. Neither you nor your agent should ever present an offer verbally; it is not considered legally binding.

Your agent will give the seller's agent your signed offer to purchase the property for a specific price, and under certain terms. This document is known as a purchase and sale agreement. It may also be called a purchase contract or a sales contract, or other terms, depending on where you live.

The purchase and sale agreement is an official document which will be used at closing. I suggest having an attorney review your offer before it's presented to the seller.

The Purchase and Sale Agreement

The Purchase and Sale Agreement document should include identification of the property, the buyer's name or names a statement of intent to purchase, the seller's name or names and a statement of intent to sell. At a minimum, the following elements should be included: (See the Standard Residential Purchase Agreement in the Appendix of this book.)

→ Legal description of the property

→ Earnest money

→ Offer price

→ Down payment

→ Financing terms

→ Personal property inclusions or exclusions

→ Closing and occupancy dates

→ Expiration date of the offer

→ Contingency requirements

Let's look at what some of these inclusions signify.

Legal Description

The address of the property, including its location and boundaries.

Earnest Money

Earnest money, or a "good faith" deposit, is submitted to the seller with the offer. This money demonstrates the buyer is serious. The amount to submit depends on what is customary in your area. Typically, the larger the purchase price of the home, the larger the earnest money check. Your agent will help you determine a fair amount of earnest money to include with your offer.

The check must be made out to an escrow company, the real estate broker, or to an attorney. It must be deposited into an escrow account until the sale of the property is either agreed upon or cancelled.

Your earnest money deposit will be returned to you in a predetermined number of days IF:

→ The seller does not accept your offer

→ Major defects are uncovered during the professional inspection

→ You cannot obtain financing

→ Specific conditions in the sales contract cannot be fulfilled

If the sale is completed, the money usually is applied toward your down payment. You risk forfeiting the earnest money if the seller accepts the contract and all the conditions of the contract have been met yet you back out.

Offer Price

The purchase agreement should also include the price you are offering and the terms and conditions under which the money will be paid. (See Financing Terms, below)

Down Payment

The amount of cash the buyer intends to put down on the home, including the earnest money deposit, is called the down payment. Your lender determined the amount of cash you will need for the down payment when you prequalified for a specific loan amount.

Financing Terms

The type of loan you will accept for the remainder of the purchase is incorporated into the agreement. The terms of the loan (rates and points) should be specified along with the maximum interest rate you are willing to pay and how long you have to find the financing terms you've specified.

Personal Property

Any personal property you want included in the transaction, or the seller wants excluded (such as refrigerator, stove, or light fixtures) should be written into, or out of, the purchase agreement. Make sure you list everything the owner is leaving on the property. Do not rely on a verbal agreement. Put it in writing!

Closing and Occupancy Dates

The date the closing is to take place and the date and time you can occupy the property must be disclosed and agreed upon by the seller and the buyer. Don't assume the dates are the same.

You can state in the purchase agreement that the seller must pay rent on a daily basis if he or she has not moved from the premises on the day of closing (or another agreed upon date). Specify how much money the seller will pay you in rent per day.

Expiration Date of the Offer

The purchase agreement should specify the length of time the offer is valid, usually three to five days.

Contingency Requirements

Contingencies, which are special conditions added to the standard terms of the purchase agreement, must be satisfied in order for the sale to be completed. Both buyers and sellers can require contingencies to the agreement. For example:

→ A buyer might present an offer to a seller contingent on the sale of another property in order to have enough cash for the down payment.

→ A seller might indicate that the sale of the house is contingent upon approval of a contract for a home they are trying to purchase.

→ The most commonly written contingencies and provisions concern financing, inspections, appraisals and title clearance.

Financing Contingency

The financing contingency states that if the buyer does not get a loan at the specified terms, the earnest money is refunded and the deal is nullified. Make sure the contingency states the terms of the loan you want:

→ Maximum interest rate you will pay

→ Discount points

→ Type of loan (such as fixed or adjustable rate)

→ Term (how many years you need to repay the loan, such as 15, 20, or 30)

This contingency protects you from being forced to accept unfavorable loan terms or forfeiting your earnest money deposit.

The seller may want a clause included in the agreement requiring that the buyer make a "good faith" effort to obtain a loan within a certain time frame. Make sure the time allotted for you to obtain a loan is reasonable.

Inspection Contingencies

Professional home inspections are highly recommended, especially for older homes. The inspection contingency protects the buyer from hidden problems with the house before the agreement goes into effect. Most conventional lenders require a termite inspection contingency. It is a requirement that FHA (Federal Housing Authority) and VA (Veterans Administration) government backed loans have termite inspections. Some common contingencies are for structural and mechanical systems, septic systems, the presence of asbestos, radon, or lead based paint, or soil contamination.

The purchase agreement should state that its validity is contingent on a satisfactory home inspection report by a professional home inspector. If the report reveals significant defects, the buyer can ask the seller to fix the problems, reduce the sales price to compensate the buyer for the costs of repairs, or void the agreement.

The seller can accept the solution, reject it, or suggest another option, such as splitting the cost of the repairs with the buyer or correcting some of them. Whatever you and the seller agree to do, put it in writing.

If you are to be reimbursed for repairs completed after closing, get repair estimates from reliable contractors. These costs can be credited to you at closing. If the inspection contingency expires before repair estimates can be collected, the seller can grant an extension to the contingency due date.

These reimbursements will appear as "credit repairs for the buyer" on the closing statement. If the seller's contribution (up to

6% of the sale) has been exhausted, the seller can reimburse the buyer for some of the repairs by cashier's checks at closing. These checks must be made out to the contractors who will do the work.

If the repairs cannot be made until after closing, some lenders will allow the seller's money to be held in escrow or trust until the repairs are complete. If agreement cannot be reached on who will pay for the repairs, you have the right to cancel the sale.

Appraisal Contingency

Your lender usually requires a professional real estate appraisal when you apply for a loan. The appraiser evaluates the property and writes an opinion about its market value. This opinion determines how large a mortgage the lender will give you. If the home is appraised at a value lower than the agreed upon purchase price, you have the right to withdraw your offer.

Clear Title

The purchase agreement should state that it is contingent on receiving clear title to the property. A title search on the property insures that the seller owns the property and that there are no liens (legal claims) against it by creditors for unpaid bills or unpaid taxes. All claims must be satisfied or paid before or at closing by the seller. The buyer pays for the title search.

Other Provisions

Write any contingency or provision you think necessary for your protection into the agreement.

Repair Work

Make sure the seller ensures all systems (heat, electric, plumbing, and mechanical) are in working order at the time of closing. If you do not include such a clause, you are agreeing to accept the house "as is."

Walk-through Inspection

Provide for a walk-through inspection of the house on the day of closing or a few days before to make sure everything is in working order and all unsatisfied conditions have been remedied.

Once you've made your initial offer, let's see how to make a counteroffer.

Negotiating the Counteroffer

In some instances, the seller will accept the offer you made. If so, you're about to own a house! In most cases, the seller will make a counteroffer, which negates the one you presented.

A counteroffer means that the seller does not accept your offer, but wants to negotiate with you. Typically, the counteroffer is below the seller's asking price but more than your initial offer. You can accept or eject it; you are not obligated to accept the counteroffer. This is where the bargaining begins!

You may go back and forth several times with the seller, making offers and receiving counteroffers, until an acceptable price is negotiated and agreed upon. Utilize your agent's experience as a guide when you're deciding how much to increase your initial offer or your most recent offer.

Make sure your counteroffers are reasonable; you want the seller to appreciate your sincere efforts to negotiate in good faith. The seller does not have to continue the negotiations and has the right to stop the process at any time.

When negotiations between you and the seller are close but at a standstill, you might suggest settling at a price somewhere between the last offer and counteroffer. Everyone feels good in a win-win situation.

If you have offered the highest price you can afford, it's all right to counteroffer with the same amount of money as the last offer. Tell the seller it's your final offer. This is a good time to negotiate settlement costs with the seller, or to consider the condition of the property and ask the seller to sell at a lower price to help pay for needed repairs, new carpeting, or other items you need to replace.

When the agreement is accepted and signed, some sellers require more money down. If this is the case, the additional deposit money is held in escrow along with your initial deposit money presented with the offer.

You Have a Deal

Now that the purchase agreement is signed you know you DON'T have to RENT anymore. You can buy, and you did! But you're not a homeowner yet.

During the next few weeks, you and the seller have plenty to do. The next chapter will take you through disclosures and the home inspection process. A professional home inspection is one of the contingencies in the purchase and sale agreement and it's vital to your becoming a first time homeowner.

Chapter Notes

1. *Barron's Dictionary of Real Estate Terms*, Third Edition.

8

CHAPTER

Disclosure and Home Inspections

The Real Estate Transfer Disclosure Statement

R eal estate law in many states requires sellers to disclose the condition of their property to the buyer. To make this information known, the seller must complete a real estate transfer disclosure statement, part of a standard real estate transaction. The seller, the buyer, and the agent(s) must acknowledge receipt of the disclosure by signing the statement.

Because lawsuits are possible if buyers discovered undisclosed property

Action	✓
Get Pre-Approved	✓
Prepare a Wish List/ Choose a Location	✓
Find an Agent	✓
Look for a Home	✓
Negotiate the Purchase	✓
Hire an Inspector	✓
Obtain a Mortgage	
Close the Deal	

defects, such as cracks in the foundation walls or leaks in the roof, prudent sellers disclose potential problems. Such disclosure—even if the defect has been repaired and is out of sight—protects the seller. If a buyer signs off on the disclosure statement that reveals the defect, little recourse can be taken later.

Exposing property defects minimizes the possibility of legal action after closing. In this chapter, you will learn about seller disclosure and the value of a home inspection.

When State Law does not require Disclosure

In states that do not require disclosure, sellers and agents often sign voluntary disclosure statements. Some real estate offices request that sellers complete disclosure forms before they list the property, even if it is not mandated by the state. In that case, you can ask the seller to complete a disclosure form by making the request a contingency of your purchase offer.

Disclosure and Government Loans

Government backed lending, such as Federal Housing Authority (FHA) loans and Housing and Urban Development (HUD) loans, requires seller disclosure regardless of state law. You will learn more about the requirements of government loans in the next chapter.

The Disclosure Form

The disclosure form (see the appendix) contains questions the seller must answer about the property, such as: Does the property have a range, dishwasher, washer, dryer, central heat, and other built in or attached appliances? Are all in operating condition? The form also asks if there are significant defects in the condition of the roof, ceilings, floors, walls, windows, doors, and more. The seller is obligated to provide complete and accurate information, including the reason for any defect and if the remedy is considered to be a minor or major repair.

An agent who represents the seller is responsible to disclose any visual defects as well and to sign off on the condition of the property.

> "The disclosure form contains questions the seller must answer about the property . . ."

Law differs from state to state regarding the seller's obligation to disclose murder, suicide, natural death, severe illness or serious crime, that could have taken place on the property. Check with your agent about applicable federal and state disclosure requirements.

As a buyer, you have the right to cancel the purchase agreement on the basis of disclosure. After the disclosure statement has been delivered to you, you have time (typically three to five days) to reject the sale. If you don't want to terminate the buying process, you can use this time to negotiate what action to take about objectionable items on the disclosure statement.

If your state does not have laws requiring disclosure, and if you are not borrowing from a government backed lender, it could be prudent for you to include a "safey net" statement in your purchase agreement. The statement would permit you to back out of the proposed sale if you find flaws in the property and to receive a full refund of your deposit, without penalty. Include in the statement a provision that gives you several days after receiving the disclosure statement to accept it or terminate the proposed purchase.

The Home Inspection

Before hiring a professional inspector, most buyers will conduct an inspection of the property to the best of their ability. The buyer may discover obvious problems that convince him or her the home

Examining the Home
- **Preliminary Inspection**
- **Professional Inspection**
- **Final Walk-Thru Inspection**

is not right. On the other hand, a house could pass your preliminary inspection yet fail a professional examination.

I suggest you do both. And don't forget that you'll have one more time to examine the house—within 24 hours of closing.

The Preliminary Home Inspection

It's important to gather as much information as you can about the condition of the home before you buy it, not after. Think of yourself as an investigator and, working with your real estate professional, complete the following three steps:

Step 1 – Interview

Tell your agent to ask the other's agent these questions:

- ❑ Is the seller aware of any termite damage in the home?

- ❑ Has the seller seen any signs of the roof leaking?

- ❑ Has the property been tested for radon?

- ❑ Has the seller made any home improvements or completed any remodeling since owning the home?

- ❑ If so, were the proper permits obtained?

- ❑ If so, when?

- ❑ If so, what improvements or remodeling was done and how much was invested in each project?

Step 2 – Examine

Conduct your own home "inspection" by looking at the applicable items:

- ❏ Basement (cracks in the walls? signs of water presence or damage?)

- ❏ Ceilings (cracks)

- ❏ Doors (hang straight, easy to open and close?)

- ❏ Drainage (run water in every sink, basin and bathtub to see if it drains quickly)

- ❏ Floors (general condition)

- ❏ Electrical Service (look at the master fuse box; can you add circuits? Are all circuit breaker spaces filled?)

- ❏ Exterior Finish (If it's brick, how's the mortar; if it's wood, how's the paint: if it's siding, what condition is it in?

- ❏ Gutters and down spouts/flashing and trim (Visible rust or breaks, puddles at the base of a downspout?)

- ❏ Fireplaces (When was the chimney last swept?)

- ❏ Foundation (any cracks or water damage visible?)

- ❏ Garage (Up to code safety garage door opener?)

- ❏ Heating, Ventilation, and Air Conditioning (HVAC) (turn everything on and off; test all thermostats)

- ❏ Kitchen and Bathrooms (Floors, tile for loose grout; faucets and shower heads for water pressure; toilets for flushing)

- ❏ Layout (Does the house "feel" comfortable to you as you walk about, and can you get from one room to another easily and conveniently?)

❑ Roof (Exterior appearance?)

❑ Walls (Interior and exterior for cracks)

❑ Windows (Check to see if all open and close easily; is the glass intact in all?)

Step 3 – Analyze

Analyze the data from your inspection.

❑ Estimate the cost for remodeling, renovation, and repairs, if done professionally

❑ Dollar value of work completed by seller

❑ Cost comparison of materials

❑ Estimate maintenance costs

If you find something wrong with the house, but you want to continue with your proposed purchase, you can ask the seller to correct the problem or adjust the asking price so you can make the necessary improvement or repair.

If you're satisfied with your preliminary analysis, consider getting a professional home inspection.

Typically, after the purchase agreement has been signed, a buyer will order a professional home inspection of the property. Your purchase agreement should contain an inspection contingency so you can hire a professional home inspection and take action based on the inspector's findings. In addition, your contingency statement should give you the right to obtain cost estimates if the inspection identifies problems you consider to be serious. The contingency should provide that your deposit money is refunded if you are not satisfied with the results of the inspection.

Ask your professional home inspector to review the seller's disclosure statement. Perhaps the seller indicated that cracks in the foundation have been repaired but cannot be seen because they're covered by wallboard. Your inspector can examine the repair site and give you an opinion about what was done and when.

A good inspector will be able to distinguish serious structural problems, if they exist, for example, from simpler problems. Remember, all houses have flaws of one kind or another. Just how severe they are is what's important now.

The Professional Home Inspection

For your protection, get a professional home inspection by a qualified inspector. This inspector will take an unbiased look at the home you wish to purchase. Professional inspections can cost between $200 and $500 or more, and should include a written report. The price depends on several factors, such as the size of the home or what is being inspected. For the fee, you should get an in-depth written evaluation of the condition of the property, including the inspector's evaluation of the structural integrity of the building, the quality of construction, and all the mechanical systems in the house.

The inspector will identify items that need to be repaired or replaced, such as windows that do not have

The Home Inspector

• Choose an inspector

• Ask for references

• Find out scope of inspection

• Request insurance coverage

• Obtain a written report

screens and doors that do not open or shut properly. The report should give an estimate of how long the major systems, equipment, structure, and finishes might last before needing replacement.

Every inspection should include evaluation of all these items, at a minimum:

→ Foundations

→ Doors and Windows

→ Roof and Siding

→ Heating and Air Conditioning Systems

→ Ceilings, Walls, and Floors

→ Insulation

→ Ventilation

→ Septic Tanks, Wells, or Sewer Lines

→ Common Areas (in condominiums or coops)

Choosing your Inspector

Hiring a competent inspector is essential. This is probably the most expensive purchase you'll ever make, so you want a highly qualified, objective and professional opinion.

Your real estate agent can recommend inspectors. You can ask your friends who recently purchased homes for referral, or you can search "Building Inspection Service" on the internet or in a local phone directory. Try to get at least three inspector's names and telephone numbers. Ask for and check references before committing to their services.

"Hiring a competent inspector is essential."

The American Society of Home Inspectors (ASHI) is a large trade association for home inspectors. The organization has strict standards for its members; they're required to be experienced inspectors and to continually improve their performance through ongoing training. They also offer insurance coverage to members. ASHI can refer you to inspectors in your area. Contact ASHI at 1-800-743-2744 or at www.ashi.com.

The National Association of Home Inspectors (NAHI) at www.nahi.org has standards similar to ASHI. I suggest you consider hiring an inspector with a membership in one of these organizations.

Here are some other possibilities:

→ Retired professionals from your local Building and Safety Department. His or her job was to inspect property for compliance with the appropriate codes.

→ Retired contractors can be an excellent choice because of their knowledge of home construction.

→ Retired structural engineers know all about the structure of a building and can analyze, diagnose and problem-solve structural solutions. Retired engineers are worth considering especially if you feel there might be a problem with the foundation of the house.

Scope of the Inspection

When hiring an inspector, make sure you ask what he or she will be inspecting, because not all inspectors are qualified to inspect all systems. If the property has a complex security system, underground sprinklers, spa, septic system, in-ground swimming pool, or other features the inspector did not mention, consider hiring a specialist—or look for someone who has expertise in all the areas you want checked.

Insurance Coverage

Make sure the inspector has errors and omissions insurance pertaining to the inspection business. If the inspector misses a defect and you find out after you purchase the house that something does not function properly, you may be able to collect damages from the inspector.

Your Role

You and your agent should plan on meeting the inspector the day of the inspection. If your inspector wants to inspect the property erty alone, arrange to meet at the house after the inspection is complete. This will give you the opportunity to see any identified problem areas the inspector has identified and to ask questions.

If the inspector has asked you to be present for the inspection, wear clothing that is appropriate for climbing in the attic and looking around the basement. This gives you the opportunity, for example, to ask if the electrical service is adequate for your kitchen appliances or home office requirements. Remember, all homes have defects of some kind, from minor cosmetic dislikes to more serious ones. Ask your inspector to tell you which are potentially more significant than others.

Typically, the homeowner is not home during the inspection, which will take two hours or more to complete.

Most inspectors take a systematic approach to their work; some start outside and go in and others start inside and go outside.

What You Will Do

- Go to the Inspection
- Observe
- Ask Questions
- Take Notes
- Review the Report with the Inspector

Outcome of the Home Inspection

Your home inspection is intended to identify problems with the property before you complete the purchase. The inspector will produce a written report summarizing the identified problems, along with possible cost estimates for replacement or repair.

If serious problems (such as an inoperable heating or air conditioning system or a cracked foundation) are identified, the written report can help you nullify your intended purchase agreement (with a full refund of your deposit) or negotiate an adjustment in the purchase price of the house. If your inspector's report identifies possible defects that require further inspection, such as a potential roof problem, I suggest you ask a roofing contractor, in this example, for an opinion. If remedial work is recommended, also ask for an estimate.

Although you've invested in the home inspection, don't be "penny wise and pound foolish" with regard to an additional investigation into mold, termite, septic system or water well-related issues. If you're serious about the house, paying for an additional service could be much cheaper that a costly repair later. If you think the subsequent inspection is too expensive, you could ask the seller to share the cost with you to save the sale.

> **". . . you have at least three opportunities to inspect the house you're considering . . ."**

If there are no significant defects noted in the inspection report, you can ask the seller to fix all or some of the minor defects before continuing with the purchase. Once you and the seller agree on all provisions of the contract, you should feel confident to shop for a loan.

Just remember you have at least three opportunities to inspect the house you're considering—your own inspection, a professioal inspection, and the final "walk through" that you complete within 24 hours of closing. We'll talk about that in Chapter Ten.

You now have a good understanding of the seller's obligation to disclose defects in the house, whether mandated by the state, your lender, or voluntarily disclosed.

And as a buyer, you know you can nullify your purchase agreement based on undisclosed or serious defects. The three opportunities for home inspection—your preliminary viewing, the professional inspection, and the final walk-thru—give you time to detect problems and resolve issues before moving ahead with the purchase.

With that kind of protection, I hope you see why I'm encouraging you to buy. Don't Rent! The next step is shopping for your loan—and I'll guide you through the process of selecting the right lender and the right mortgage program for you in the next chapter.

Obtain a Mortgage

Shopping, Comparing and Negotiating

Obtaining a loan is a three-step process: Shopping for the best terms, comparing all the information you'll receive, and then negotiating the mortgage loan that's best—for you. While time is of the essence—recall that clause in your purchase agreement which gives you a certain amount of time to obtain a mortgage loan—I urge you to proceed carefully and cautiously. Because you're pre-qualified, you're in an excellent position to shop, compare and negotiate. Your task now is to gather all the information you'll need to do that.

Action	✓
Get Pre-Approved	✓
Prepare a Wish List/ Choose a Location	✓
Find an Agent	✓
Look for a Home	✓
Negotiate the Purchase	✓
Hire an Inspector	✓
Obtain a Mortgage	✓
Close the Deal	

As you begin this step in the process toward becoming a first time homeowner, you should know:

The Equal Credit Opportunity Act[1] prohibits lenders form discriminating against credit applicants in any aspect of a credit transaction on the basis of race, color, religion, national origin, sex, marital status, age, whether all or part of the applicant's income is derived from a public assistance program or whether the applicant has in good faith exercised a right under the Consumer Credit Protection Act.

The Fair Housing Act[2] prohibits discrimination in residential real estate transactions on the basis of race, color, religion, sex, handicap, familial status, or national origin. Under these laws, a consumer cannot be refused a loan based on these characteristics nor be charged more for a loan or offered less favorable terms based on such characteristics.

In this chapter, we're going to review the three sets of choices you're going to make on your way to becoming a homeowner:

→ Will you work with a mortgage lender or a mortgage broker?

→ Do you want a fixed rate or adjustable rate mortgage?

→ What combination of interest rate, points, closing costs and other financial factors is most favorable to you?

As you begin, I want you to avoid two common mistakes that many first time homebuyers make in their eagerness to become first time homeowners.

First: Recall that I encouraged you to interview a number of potential real estate agents before selecting one. The same is true with lenders. Interview as many as you like, but select one.

Second: Recall that I encouraged you to get pre-approved from a mortgage originator before you begin home shopping. Start the pre-approval process after you've selected a mortgage lender. Here's why: Each loan application you submit triggers an inquiry to the major credit reporting bureaus; excessive credit inquiries frequently indicate credit problems, which can result in a lower credit score. It is to your advantage to trigger as few credit-related inquiries as possible.

Mortgage Lender or a Mortgage Broker?

Your choices are a mortgage banker—the actual lender—or a mortgage broker, a go-between, or middleman, between you and your lender. The mortgage banker will loan you the money to buy your first home. The mortgage broker, who acts on your behalf as a "match-maker", will shop your loan application with a number of lenders to find a suitable match, and to earn a fee for doing so.

To help you choose a mortgage banker or broker, I suggest you ask for a referral from friends, family and coworkers who have bought a home recently. An outstanding reputation is often the best referral. If making such an inquiry is not practical, local real estate offices, newspaper advertisements and the internet can be helpful.

> **"An outstanding reputation is often the best referral."**

When you meet with recommended resources, tell them about your desire to become a first-time homeowner. Listen carefully to how eager they seem to be to work with you. Ask about their professional certifications or designations.

Some mortgage brokers prefer to work with experienced buyers, or with buyers in certain income brackets. As a mortgage broker, I've always enjoyed working with first time buyers; helping them through their initial anticipation and then sharing their excitement when we close on their new home is a unique and special thrill for me.

You can make the lender versus broker decision after you know more about the kind of mortgage you want and the total costs, short and long term, involved. As you do your research, get information from both; you don't need to make a commitment to either one at this initial stage. Much of your research, in fact, will help you decide what is most important: Where *you* can get the most favorable mortgage.

I suggest you start at the bank or financial institution where you have your savings, checking and money market accounts. Ask if the organization makes or brokers residential mortgages. Don't stop there, however. Mortgages are a highly competitive business today, so do yourself a huge financial favor and investigate every possible source: a mortgage broker, your credit union, professional or trade associations you belong to, the financial services firm that manages your mutual fund or retirement accounts, state and regional housing agencies, private home financing companies—or even the seller.

> **"The local Better Business Bureau can tell you if complaints about the mortgage banker or broker are on file."**

Some mortgage brokers guarantee their fees at the beginning; this avoids you learning the broker's costs at closing. Visit www.mtgprofessor.com for more information about these organizations and their business practices, which include disclosing the wholesale cost of the mortgages they sell.

You should know that all mortgage bankers are subject to regulation at local, state and federal levels. To learn how the industry is regulated in your state, contact either the state's department of banking or division of real estate. The Library of Congress has an index of state and local government web sites.

Not all states require mortgage brokers to be licensed, so check with the appropriate department or bureau of your state government. The local Better Business Bureau can tell you if complaints about the mortgage banker or broker are on file. Such professional organizations as a local Association of Mortgage Brokers can provide information about its members.

An important caution:

Avoid becoming a victim of predatory lending

Most mortgage lenders and brokers have your best interests in mind. However, there are "predatory lenders" who act unscrupulously and may try to take advantage of you. Although predatory lending is not defined by federal law, and states define it differently, this type of lending usually involves loans with terms you can't meet - no matter how good the deal sounds - and practices that strip away the equity in your home.

Who do predatory lenders target?

Predatory lenders target people who may have fewer credit choices or are perceived as higher credit risks. Predatory lenders usually reach out to elderly and low-income homebuyers, minorities and women, people with less than perfect credit, and people who know very little about home loans and mortgages. These lenders usually tell you that you can get loans with very low monthly payments, refinance your existing mortgage, or take out a loan or second mortgage to help pay for expenses like medical costs and home-improvement work.

How can you spot a predatory lender?

Predatory lenders usually offer loans with high interest rates; broker fees; unnecessary costs like pre-paid life insurance; and unaffordable repayment terms.

Be suspicious of anyone who offers you "bargain loans," whether they mail or E-mail you an offer, call you on the phone, or come to your door. Avoid promises of "No Credit? Bad Credit? No Problem!" and beware of offers that are only "good for a very short time."

Avoid lenders who encourage you to borrow more than you need or more than the value of the home. Beware of terms that change at the last minute or offer next-day approval based on your making prepayments or paying up-front fees.

"Packing" a loan with single premium credit insurance products, such as credit life insurance, and not adequately disclosing the inclusion, cost or any additional fees associated with the insurance.

Charging excessive rates and fees to a borrower who qualifies for lower rates and/or fees offered by the lender.

Repeatedly refinancing a loan within a short period of time and charging high points and fees with each refinance.

If you suspect you have been approached by a predatory lender, or have entered into some negotiations or agreements with a suspected predatory lender, contact local, state or federal regulators.

Mortgage Banker

As I noted, the mortgage banker is the lender and the lender makes the ultimate credit decision. This could mean a faster decision, and you won't pay any finder's fees or commissions. However, a mortgage banker will present you with only that lender's mortgage products. My advice: Talk to several to get comparative information. Interest rates, qualification standards and other factors will vary from one mortgage banker to another. You can find the names of mortgage bankers listed in your local telephone book or newspaper, and you can search the internet for sources, too.

Mortgage Broker

A mortgage broker is a specialist in matching the needs of borrowers with the unique programs of a large number of lenders.

> "... the broker selects a mortgage lender who, in the broker's opinion, is most likely to accept your application."

Unlike the mortgage banker, who can show you a limited number of options, a mortgage broker can draw from a large pool of lenders to find the right match. In some cases, the mortgage broker is a lender, too.

There's another advantage, too. A mortgage broker acquainted with the special programs of many different lenders is in a position to help you if you have special needs. The mortgage broker completes the same tasks as the mortgage banker, such as checking your credit and work record, arranging for title search and hiring a property appraiser. When your file is complete, the broker selects a mortgage lender who, in the broker's opinion, is most likely to accept your application. My advice here is the same as dealing with mortgage bankers: Talk to several—or ask the broker you're working with to show you options from several sources, or several options from the same lender.

Which is better? That depends on the mortgage package you negotiate, which depends to a large extent on the strength of your mortgage application. You don't need to make a decision about a broker or lender at this point.

Approach every prospective lender with a concise, accurate statement of what you want. The language is in your purchase agreement: The address of the property, your credit score, the amount and percentage down payment you plan to make and the kind of mortgage you're interested in (fixed or adjustable rate, with no points). Ask what kind of rates the lender is offering now, and what its fees are.

> **"A fixed rate mortgage locks in the amount of your monthly principal and interest payment for the life of your loan."**

To help you compare mortgage programs, here is the internet address of the Department of Housing and Urban Development's pamphlet "Looking for the Best Mortgage." I'd suggest you use or copy the very helpful Mortgage Shopping Worksheet at the back of the HUD booklet at:

http://www.hud.gov/utilities/intercept.cfm?/buying/booklet.pdf

Fixed Rate or Adjustable Rate Mortgage?

In addition to the interest rate you will pay, there is another important factor in deciding between a fixed rate or adjustable rate mortgage: How long you think you'll live in the property you want to buy.

I'll review some special mortgage programs later in this chapter. Right now, let's focus on fixed rate and adjustable rate mortgages.

If you plan on staying in the house a long time—more than seven years, which is the average length of residency for homebuyers today—look at fixed rate mortgage programs. A **fixed rate mortgage** locks in the amount of your monthly principal and interest payment for the life of your loan. The only change in your monthly payment will occur if your property taxes and insurance increase or decrease.

If you plan on staying in the house for less than seven years—say two or three years—you'll probably want to evaluate an **adjustable rate mortgage**, known as an ARM in the industry. ARMs usually have lower interest rates in the first several years, to keep your monthly payments lower. The lower monthly payment also allows you to qualify for a larger mortgage. (Recall the income-to-payment ratios discussed in chapter 3.) After a period of time—usually one, three or five years—the interest rate can be adjusted; if it goes up, your monthly payment probably will increase. If interest rates decline, your monthly payment could be decreased.

But don't base your choice solely on the quoted interest rates of available fixed- or adjustable-rate mortgages. This step demands careful research, thorough data keeping and your willingness to complete the rigorous process of gathering, compiling and analyzing detailed information from every lender you talk with—mortgage banker or broker.

Let's look at the information you will need, and why it's so essential to your making an informed decision that's best for you. While some of the costs and fees are not payable until you close—a subject we'll discuss in the next chapter—I want you to have a full understanding of ALL the fees and costs associated with your mortgage. I don't want you to be surprised (or, even worse, shocked) at the "extras" you didn't know about until closing. Here's a quick review of the costs and fees to ask about when you're shopping for your mortgage. Remember: Your monthly mortgage payment, for interest and principal only, is one of the factors to consider in arriving at and evaluating the *total cost* of your mortgage.

Ask each prospective lender about each of these factors and enter them into your mortgage comparison worksheet.

Discount Points

Discount points are fees the lender charges, based on the amount of money you borrow for your mortgage. You can expect to negotiate a lower interest rate on your mortgage by paying more discount points; each point is worth one percent of your mortgage. For example, three points charged on a $200,000 mortgage loan is calculated by multiplying 3 (the number of points) x .01 (one percent, expressed as a decimal) x $200,000 (the amount of money being borrowed) = $6,000. Typically, the buyer pays points in cash at closing.

> **"You can expect to negotiate a lower interest rate on your mortgage by paying more discount points…"**

Loan Origination Fees

These fees, payable by the buyer, are assessed by the lender. They're charges for originating and processing the loan and in many case are expressed as a percentage of the loan amount. Like points, they're payable at closing.

Interest rate

Most frequently, you will see two rates quoted: The interest rate and the APR, or Annual Percentage Rate. The interest rate is the cost of borrowing mortgage money, expressed as a percentage rate. If you're buying a $250,000 house, for example, and make a 20% down payment ($50,000), you're borrowing $200,000 ($250,000-$50,000). Depending on the discount points and fees the lender charges, the total cost of borrowing is higher and will be expressed in the APR.

Transaction, Settlement or Closing Costs

A number of fees or costs can be included, including fees for processing your application, legal fees, appraisal, credit report, survey, recording and notary services; title examination, abstract and insurance; and document preparation fees for deeds, mortgages and settlement statements. Under provisions of the federal Real Estate Settlement Procedures Act, you will receive a "good faith" estimate of your closing costs when you apply for a mortgage or within three days of your application. Each cost will be listed as an amount or a range.

> "... you will receive a 'good faith' estimate of your closing costs when you apply for a mortgage ..."

Mortgage Insurance

There are two types of mortgage insurance products that indirectly benefit homebuyers.

→ Private Mortgage Insurance (PMI) for private loans (also called conventional loans)

→ Mortgage Insurance Premiums (MIP) for government backed loans

Low down payment loans are considered risky to lenders because they go into default more often. If a homebuyer does not have a lot of personal money invested, it makes it easier to walk away during economic hard times. These mortgage insurance protection policies guarantee the lender re-payment of a percentage of the loan if the homeowner defaults.

PMI and MIP are not insurance policies to protect you; they were developed to protect the lender. These policies allow lenders to approve loans they wouldn't normally consider—loans with lower down payments.

Private Mortgage Insurance

Known as PMI, private mortgage insurance protects the lender against loss if the borrower is unable to pay and defaults on the loan. PMI is usually required if your down payment is less than 20% of the purchase price. In fact, you can finance a house with a lender with as little as 3 to 5 percent down provided you purchase Private Mortgage Insurance (PMI).

The premium for your PMI will be added to your monthly payment. A five percent down payment on a $200,000 loan is now $10,000 if you purchase a protection policy for the lender. It might not be quite as difficult to save for a 3-5% down payment, will it?

> "Mortgage Insurance Premiums are required in order to obtain a low down payment government-backed loan. . ."

Mortgage Insurance Premiums

Mortgage Insurance Premiums (MIP) are required in order to obtain a low down payment government-backed loan. These insurance policies permit lenders to loan money for houses that otherwise would be too risky to consider.

If you are considering a low down payment private/conventional loan, the cost of the PMI premium can be waived (if you request it) when the loan balance gets to 78% or less of the home's market value. At that time, the lender will view you as having a vested interest in your home.

However, if you have a low down payment government backed loan, it is unlikely you will get the MIP waived without refinancing the home again. You should consider refinancing when the loan balance falls below 80% of the home's market value. If that occurs, you may be eligible for a refund of part of the upfront[2] MIP (UFMIP) you paid.

To find out if you are eligible for a refund, call your local office of the U.S. Department of Housing and Urban Development (HUD) to inquire.

Upfront fees are associated with mortgage insurance. This upfront insurance premium can be financed at the time of the purchase. Some monthly premiums are added to your regular mortgage payment. Check with your lender or go to www.hud.gov for up-to-date information.

Here's a table you can use to determine what kind of mortgage program or programs you're qualified for. Once you know that, you can utilize the resources presented later in this chapter, or in the appendix, to get all the details.

If . . .	You might qualify for . . .
You're a first time home buyer ...	The homeownership voucher program that helps you convert monthly rental payments to mortgage payments. If that sounds like a program you'd be interested in, take a look at www.hud.gov for more information. You might also qualify for municipal, county or state housing authority special financial assistance programs. Talk to your lender or real estate agent.
You served in the United States Armed Forces ...	A Veterans Administration (VA) loan. Veterans seeking more detailed information concerning the VA home loan program may request VA Pamphlet 26-4, VA-Guaranteed Home Loans for Veterans, or VA Pamphlet 26-6, To the Homebuying Veteran, from the nearest VA office. Loan Guaranty personnel at that office will also be pleased to answer specific questions and provide other assistance.

If . . .	You might qualify for . . .
	VA-guaranteed financing is a benefit which Congress intended for eligible veterans. If you are a veteran and a home buyer, it makes sense to look into the VA loan program as a good way to finance a home purchase. To locate a VA facility, or to obtain more information on the VA Loan Guaranty program, visit www.va.gov and click on Facilities Locator. Your local VA regional office may be reached by dialing 1-800-827-1000.
If you're a law enforcement/ police officer, firefighter or emergency medical technician . . .	HUD's Good Neighbor Next Door and the Officer Next Door Program are efforts to build stronger communities and safer neighborhoods; HUD offers this program to law enforcement officers. To participate, you need to be a sworn law enforcement officer employed full time at the federal, state, county or local level. Officers working for public or private colleges and universities are eligible. You do not have to be a first time home buyer to participate in this program; however, you cannot own any other home at the time of closing. The properties are single family homes that are located in certain revitalization areas throughout the country. The program is run over the Internet. Its advantage is participating officers can purchase these homes at a 50% discount from their listing price. In addition, the officer may be eligible for certain FHA-insured mortgage programs. Go to http://www.fanniemae.com/ homebuyers/findamortgage/mortgages/mycommu nity.jhtml
If you're a teacher . . .	The Teacher Next Door Program is also offered by HUD and works the exact same way as the Officer Next Door Program except it is offered to teachers. This program encourages teachers to buy homes in designated revitalization areas. To be eligible, you must be a teacher employed full time by an educational agency serving the school district in which the home is located. Educational agencies include public and private schools at the federal, state, county or local level. The teacher must be a state certified teacher or administrator for kindergarten though 12th grade.

If . . .	You might qualify for . . .
If you need help with your down payment . . .	The American Dream Dream Downpayment Initiative (ADDI) was signed into law in late 2003 and expired in 2008. The ADDI program was created to help low-income first time homebuyers to purchase new homes by providing funding for down payments, closing costs, and some rehabilitation projects. To determine if ADDI or other homeowning assistance is available in your area, contact your local Home administering agency.
If you need help with mortgage insurance . . .	If you buy a home, HUD also has a mortgage insurance program for qualifying individuals. The mortgage must be obtained from a private lending institution such as a bank, savings and loan or traditional mortgage company. Under this program, the mortgage will be insured by HUD. Eligibility requirements for this program include: • Meeting the FHA credit qualifications. • Eligibility for 97% financing and upfront mortgage premiums can be incorporated into the mortgage itself. • Borrowers are responsible for paying annual insurance premiums. Limits apply to mortgages in each state; for more information on this program in your state, visit HUD's mortgage insurance website.

These programs are subject to change, of course, so check with the appropriate government agency. If your income to debt ratio exceeds conventional limits (28/36, as I described in chapter 3) look for more lenient FHA programs that provide loans where your debt ratio can be 29/41.

Here's a guide to home loans, including descriptions at http://www.hud.gov/offices/hsg/sfh/buying/glossary.cfm.

Type	Description
Amortized loan	A loan which provides that some of each payment goes toward repaying the principal, or the amount borrowed.
Adjustable rate mortgage (ARM)	A mortgage loan with an interest rate which can be adjusted at specified periods, up or down, depending upon a specific index or indexes. Monthly payments can vary as the interest rate is changed.
Balloon Mortgage	A mortgage that typically offers low rates for an initial period of time (usually 5, 7, or 10) years; after that time period elapses, the balance is due or is refinanced by the borrower.
Conforming Loan	A loan which conforms to Fannie Mae or Freddie Mac loan standards for the maximum loan amount.
Conventional Loan	A private sector loan not guaranteed or insured by the U.S. government.
15-Year mortgage	A loan with monthly payments calculated to pay off the total of the amount borrowed and interest in 15 years.
Fixed rate mortgage	A mortgage with payments that remain the same throughout the life of the loan because the interest rate and other terms are fixed and do not change.
Hybrid mortgage	The term includes a variety of "two-step" loans that often combine the features of adjustable and fixed rate mortgages. The loan begins with a low, fixed rate for a specified period of time. It can change to a second adjustable or fixed rate at that point.
Interest-only mortgage	A loan which provides that each payment is for interest only on the amount borrowed. The principal is not reduced, as it is with an amortized loan.

Type	Description
Jumbo Loan	A loan amount which exceeds the maximum loan limits set by Fannie Mae or Freddie Mac is considered a Jumbo loan.
Rehabilitation Mortgage	A mortgage that covers the costs of rehabilitating (repairing or improving) a property; some rehabilitation mortgages—like the FHA's 203(k)—allow a borrower to roll the costs of rehabilitation and home purchase into one mortgage loan.
30-year Mortgage	A loan with monthly payments calculated to pay off the total of the amount borrowed and interest in 30 years.
40-year Mortgage	A loan with monthly payments calculated to pay off the total of the amount borrowed and interest in 40 years.

The "1003" Application

If you've been following my home buying steps, you've completed the mortgage loan application process at least once to gain your pre-approval status. If you have not, but you've entered into a contract to buy that dream house, you must act quickly to secure a mortgage loan.

Either way, let's take a closer look at what is involved in applying for a loan and what happens from your initial application until the final approval is granted and the lender is ready to fund and close the deal.

Remember the lender is trying to establish your identity as the borrower, get a two-year history of your employment and residence, and determine your financial capability to repay your loan in full and on time.

The loan officer will need to complete the standardized mortgage loan application known as the 1003 (ten-o-three). It includes:

Section I: Type of Mortgage and Terms of Loan

Section II: Property Information and Purpose of Loan

Section III: Borrower Information

Section IV: Employment Information

Section V: Monthly Income and Combined Household Expense Information

Section VI: Assets and Liabilities

Section VII: Details of Transaction

Section VIII: Declarations

Section IX: Acknowledgement and Agreement

Section X: Information for Government Monitoring Purposes

The loan officer you're working with will collect this information and document your income and asset statements; this includes a credit report. As I've noted, you'll be charged a fee for this document. If you're pre-approved, this step has been completed.

Disclosures

Your lender is required by law to provide you with the following documents:

→ **Truth-in-Lending disclosure**. This disclosure includes a summary of the total cost of credit, such as the Annual Percentage Rate (APR) and other specifics of the loan. This is the cost of credit expressed as a yearly rate.

→ **"A Home Buyer's Guide to Settlement Costs."** This guide is a government publication that describes the closing or "settlement" process, associated costs, and your rights.

→ **Adjustable-Rate Mortgage (ARM) disclosure**. This disclosure includes information about terms and costs associated with an ARM, past performance of the index to which the interest rate will be tied, and the "Consumer Handbook on Adjustable-Rate Mortgages."

→ **GFE**. A good faith estimate is an itemized list of fees and costs associated with your loan. Your mortgage lender or broker must provide the GFE to you within three business days of applying for a loan. The estimate must include all expected expenses associated with your loan—settlement or closing costs, inspections, title insurance, taxes and other charges. Remember that it is an estimate; take it with you to your closing and question any major variation. You can use the GFE (see appendix C) to compare mortgage programs from different lenders, using the chart on page 3 of the form. You can see the form at:
http://www.hud.gov/offices/hsg/rmra/res/gfestimate.pdf

→ **Financing Agreement**. The Financing Agreement details the terms of the loan, including rate, duration, type and the distribution of funds, including compensation paid to participating agents and organizations.

→ **Appraisal**. The appraisal, which will be conducted by an independent residential property appraiser, will establish a value for the property you want to buy, based on its condition, comparable properties in the neighborhood and market dynamics. It can be more or less than the price you have negotiated. You'll be charged a fee for this service. The loan officer will likely collect this fee in advance. Otherwise, it will be included in your closing costs.

Your lender will verify your personal information.

Your bank account and employment information will be verified. Your lender may ask you for your two most recent monthly bank statements or pay stubs. If you can't provide them, a Verification of Employment (VOE) and Verification of Deposit (VOD) will be requested of your employer and banking institution to verify your last two years of employment and banking history.

Your banking information can include data about your savings, investment and retirement accounts. You also will be asked to provide copies of your federal income tax returns and information about your long term debts—obligations which will not be paid in full within the next 12 months. Your lender also can ask for information about any supplemental income you earn, adverse credit reports and payments you must make for child support or alimony.

Title Search and Title Insurance

Title insurance protects the lender's financial interest in your house and land against loss caused by title defects, liens or other matters.

Property Insurance

Property insurance protects against damages to your house caused by such hazards as fire, theft and some weather damage.

Underwriting

Underwriting is the credit analysis conducted by the lender before your mortgage is issued. It is based on the credit and work history information you provided, your bank and outher financial statements, your credit scores and the lender's assessment of your ability to repay the loan.

Chapter Notes

1. http://www.ftc.gov/bcp/edu/pubs/consumer/credit/cre15.shtm
2. http://www.usdoj.gov/crt/housing/housing_coverage.htm

Close the Deal

The Real Estate Settlement Process

You're ready now for the last step in this journey you're making toward realizing the American Dream: Home ownership. I'll summarize it for you in one word: details!

This is the concluding step in the largest financial transaction you will ever make and you're going to be signing a number of legally binding documents. It's essential that you know what you're signing and why. If you've not worked with an attorney during your home-buying process, I encourage you to do one of two things: 1. Hire a real estate attorney to review all your

Action	✓
Get Pre-Approved	✓
Prepare a Wish List/ Choose a Location	✓
Find an Agent	✓
Look for a Home	✓
Negotiate the Purchase	✓
Hire an Inspector	✓
Obtain a Mortgage	✓
Close the Deal	✓

closing documents; or 2. Ask a real estate attorney to attend the closing with you, if that's appropriate. Much of the paperwork that's been prepared—from your initial application to your commitment letter, lock-in rate verification, RESPA forms and other documents—will move front and center in the closing process. It must be legally complete and accurate. And you must understand *exactly* what you are signing. You'll also need a cashier's check or a certified check in the exact amount needed to complete the purchase—and to become a homeowner for the first time!

I'll devote the rest of this chapter to the details.

The closing, or settlement as it's called in some locales, varies from place to place. It's not unusual to have the process conducted by lenders, title insurance companies, escrow companies, real estate brokers or attorneys for you or the seller. As a result, you might be able to save some money by shopping for a settlement agent. Ask your real estate agent to describe the process in your area. If it's appropriate, then, make some phone calls to learn how much different organizations or individuals charge. I've included a copy of the HUD-1 Settlement Statement for you to use when you're shopping for settlement services; their costs can increase the cost of your loan, so shop carefully and aggressively.

". . . you must understand exactly what you are signing."

In many cases, you, the buyer, and the seller will attend the closing, along with your attorneys, the real estate agent or agents involved in the transactions and others. If the settlement is to be conducted by an escrow agent, neither you nor the seller needs to attend; both of you will sign an escrow agreement requiring that you give specified documents and funds to the agent. Because this is your first closing, however, I strongly suggest you attend so you can witness the entire process—and leave with the keys to your new home (and the garage door opener) firmly in hand.

Recall that when you applied for your mortgage loan, you might have received an "Affiliated Business Arrangement Disclosure". Businesses that provide settlement services, and which are owned or controlled by another related firm, such as a lender or title insurer, are known as "affiliates." If you received this form, it means that your lender, real estate broker, or other participant in your transaction has referred you to such a firm. You are generally not required to use the affiliate (check with an attorney) so you can shop for other providers.

Your lender *was required* to provide you with a Good Faith Estimate (see chapter 9) of settlement service charges you could expect to pay. Note that these are estimates and it's possible the actual charges you will see at closing will be different. For that reason, bring your Good Faith Estimate with you, to compare it with the final settlement costs. Ask your lender about any changes.

> **"Before closing, you will want to conduct a final walk-through of the home you're buying."**

Before closing, you will want to conduct a final walk-through of the home you're buying. If it's new construction, you will inspect the property with a representative of the builder, pointing out items which are damaged, not complete or do not meet the terms of your purchase contract.

If you're buying an existing home, you and your agent will conduct the walk through. You will want to make sure all the terms of your purchase contract have been met, such as property left on the premises or removed as well as the overall condition of the home.

On the day before your closing, you have the right to inspect the HUD-1 Settlement Statement, which lists all the services provided to you and the fees charged to you. The form is completed by the agent who will conduct the settlement, so if you want to inspect the document, make sure you know how to contact the settlement agent.

In most cases, the completed HUD-1 Settlement Statement must be delivered or mailed to you *at or before* closing. If you've decided to use an escrow agent, the HUD-1 statement will be mailed to you after closing. You have the right to review it one day before settlement.

Itemized Settlement Costs

Section L of the HUD-1 Settlement Statement contains an itemized list of the services which you might be required to pay for. A sample of the HUD-1 form is included for your reference. (Appendix C)

Let's take a look, using the line numbers on the HUD form as a reference:

> **700. Sales/Broker's Commission**: The total dollar amount of the real estate broker's sales commission, usually paid by the seller. It's usually a percentage of the negotiated selling price of the home.
>
> 700. TOTAL SALES/BROKER'S COMMISSION based on price
>
> Paid From Borrower's Funds At Settlement
>
> Paid From Seller's Funds At Settlement
>
> **800. Items Payable in Connection with Loan**: Fees lenders charge to process, approve and make the mortgage loan.
>
> **801. Loan Origination:** Usually called a loan origination fee, a "point" or "points." It's designed to compensate for the lender's administrative costs in processing the loan and is usually calculated as a percentage of the loan. It varies from lender to lender but is paid by the buyer, unless negotiated otherwise.
>
> **802. Loan Discount**: Called "points" or "discount points," a loan discount is a one-time charge imposed by the lender or

broker to lower the rate at which the lender or broker offers the loan to you. Each "point" is equal to one percent of the mortgage amount. For example, if a lender charges two points on a $200,000 loan, you will pay discount points of $4,000.

803. Appraisal Fee: For the appraiser's report.

804. Credit Report Fee: For your credit report.

805. Lender's Inspection Fee: Covers inspections made by the lender's employees or others. (Inspections made by other companies are shown in line 1302.)

806. Mortgage Insurance Application Fee: For processing your application for mortgage insurance, if required.

807. Assumption Fee: For "assuming" or taking over the seller's existing mortgage loan.

808. Mortgage Broker Fee: To a mortgage broker or brokers.

900. Items Required by Lender to Be Paid in Advance: Your lender may require that you pay such fees or costs as accrued interest, mortgage insurance premiums and hazard insurance premiums at closing.

901. Interest: Usually, your lender will require that you pay the interest on your mortgage loan that accrues, or accumulates, from the date of your closing to the end of the month.

902. Mortgage Insurance Premium: Your lender may require you to pay the first one or two months' mortgage insurance premium in advance or a lump sum premium that covers the life of the loan at closing.

903. Hazard Insurance Premium: Your lender may require you to bring to the closing either proof of your first year's hazard insurance policy, fully paid, or to pay the first year's premium at closing. The policy protects you and the lender against loss due to fire, windstorm, and natural hazards.

904. Flood Insurance: If your lender requires flood insurance, it usually will be listed here.

1000 - 1008. Escrow Account Deposits: Taxes, insurance and other items must be paid at closing to establish an escrow account. Your lender cannot collect more than a certain amount, but individual item deposits might overstate the amount that can be collected. The "aggregate adjustment" on line 1008, which will be zero or a negative amount, corrects the total due.

1100. Title Charges: Title charges, which can pay for a number of services provided by title companies and others, may not include all the listed items. It is not unusual for items not listed to be included.

1101. Settlement or Closing Fee: Paid to the closing agent or escrow holder, this fee can be paid by the seller or buyer. Negotiate with your seller to determine who will pay and how much.

1102-1104. Abstract of Title Search, Title Examination, Title Insurance Binder: Charges shown here are for the title search and examination.

1105. Document Preparation: Your lender or title company might charge a fee for the preparation of final legal papers, such as a mortgage, deed of trust, note or deed.

1106. Notary Fee: A notary public will swear that the persons named in the documents you signed are those persons, and you will pay a fee for this service.

1107. Attorney's Fees: Your lender may require that you pay for legal services provided to the lender, such as an examination of the title binder. If so, the fee will appear on this part of the form, or on lines 1111, 1112 or 1113. It is possible that the seller will agree to pay part of this fee. The cost of your attorney and/or the seller's attorney can appear here, too.

1108. Title Insurance: This shows the total cost of owner's and lender's title insurance.

1109. Lender's Title Insurance: This shows the cost of the lender's policy.

1110. Owner's (Buyer's) Title Insurance: This shows the cost of the owner's policy.

1200. Government Recording and Transfer Charges: Depending upon the contract you negotiated, these fees will be paid by you or the seller. Usually, you as buyer pay for legally recording the new deed and mortgage (line 1201). In some places, transfer taxes, which are set by state and/or local governments, are collected whenever property changes hands or a mortgage loan is made. It is not unusual to require the purchase of city, county and/or state tax stamps, as indicated on lines 1202 and 1203.

1300. Additional Settlement Charges:

1301. Survey: Your lender may require a property survey be done by a professional surveyor; this protects you and the lender. Usually, you as buyer will pay the surveyor's fee, but it's possible to negotiate payment with the seller.

1302. Pest and Other Inspections: This pays for inspections for termites or other pests in your home.

1303-1305. Lead-Based Paint Inspections: This pays for inspections or evaluations for lead-based paint hazard risk assessments (in houses built before 1978) and may be on any blank line in the 1300 series.

1400. Total Settlement Charges: All the fees you will pay are in the "Paid from Borrower's Funds at Settlement" column. The sum is transferred to line 103 of Section J, "Settlement charges to borrower" in the *Summary of Borrower's Transaction* on page 1 of the HUD-1 Settlement Statement and added to the purchase price. All the settlement fees paid by the seller are transferred to line 502 of Section K, *Summary of Seller's Transaction* on page 1 of the HUD-1 Settlement Statement.

1400. TOTAL SETTLEMENT CHARGES

Paid Outside Of Closing ("POC"): It's possible that some fees listed on the HUD-1 to the left of the borrower's column will be marked "P.O.C." meaning they are paid outside of closing. Usually, you as buyer pay before closing for credit reports and appraisals; they're an additional cost to you. Other fees, including those paid by the lender to a mortgage broker or other settlement service providers, can be paid after closing/settlement. Such fees usually are included in the interest rate or other closing charges. They are not an additional cost to you and are not included in the total on Line 1400.

The first page of the HUD-1 Settlement Statement summarizes the buyer's and seller's costs and adjustments. Section J summarizes the borrower's transaction and Section K the seller's side. While you can receive a copy of the seller's side, it is not required.

Section 100 summarizes your costs, including the contract cost of the house, any personal property you're purchasing and the total settlement charges you owe as shown in Section L.

Beginning at line 106, adjustments are made for such items as taxes and assessments that the seller paid for before the transaction was completed. If you will benefit after closing from the seller's prepayment of these items, you can expect to repay the seller for that portion of the cost.

Such as adjustment for property taxes and other expenses are itemized in Sections J and K of the HUD-1 Settlement Statement.

Here is a brief example: Property taxes, which are paid annually, will not be paid when your closing occurs on October 1. You will be required to pay the full year's taxes on December 1. However, the seller lived in the house for the first nine months of the year and will be responsible for three-fourths (9/12ths) of the year's taxes.

In the same way, you will make adjustments for other pre-paid or annual costs or fees, such as homeowner association dues, special assessments and utilities. It's important that you and the seller agree on *all* these cost sharing or prorated adjustments *before* closing. A disagreement at closing could jeopardize your purchase or cause additional expenses if your sales contract must be revised or you cannot close that day.

I suggest you notify all the utility companies serving the house of the change in ownership at least a week in advance of your closing. Request a reading on the day of closing; the bill should be sent to the seller's new address or to the closing agent. Doing so will help you avoid the unpleasant task of paying your seller's old utility bills and then attempting to collect them from the seller later.

The last thing you'll do, after you've signed all the documents and given your check to the closing agent, is get the keys to your new house.

Congratulations . . . you're a homeowner! You'll never pay rent again!

The six appendices I've prepared provide important additional information and a guide to supplementary resources that can help you achieve your goal of home ownership. They include:

A. A guide to credit reporting agencies and advice from the Federal Trade Commission about how to repair your credit.

B. A review of Fannie Mae, Freddie Mac, HUD and other federal programs

C. A reprint of Good Faith Estimate Form (GFE) and HUD-1 RESPA Settlement Statement Form

D. A reprint of a standard residential sales contract

E. A list of state agencies offering housing programs and counseling services for first-time home buyers

F. A list of key internet information resources

You will also find a glossary of acronyms, phrases, terms and words you're likely to encounter as you become a homeowner.

In addition, I encourage you to visit my website, www.dontrent.com—it's updated regularly with helpful information you can use as you master the process of becoming a homeowner.

Feel free to ask questions, make suggestions or share your experiences with me!

Good luck.
Eddie Fadel

APPENDIX

How to Contact Credit Reporting Agencies

You can contact the three major credit reporting agencies by mail, telephone or internet. Their addresses are:

Equifax
P.O. Box 740241
Atlanta, GA 30374
1-800-685-1111
www.equifax.com

Experian
P.O. Box 2002
Allen, TX 75013
1 888 397 3742
www.experian.com

TransUnion
P.O. Box 1000
Chester, PA 19022
1-800-888-4213
www.transunion.com

To Request your Credit Report Online

The Fair & Accurate Credit Transactions Act of 2004 entitles you to a free copy of your credit report from all three credit bureaus once a year. Visit www.annualcreditreport.com.

To Request your Credit Report by Phone

Call 1-877-322-8228 to request your credit reports by phone. You will go through a simple verification process over the phone. Your reports will be mailed to you.

To Request your Credit Report by Mail

You can request your credit report by mail by filling out the request form and mailing it to:

Annual Credit Report Request Service
P.O. Box 105281
Atlanta , GA 30348-528

How to Repair Your Credit[1]

CREDIT REPAIR: SELF-HELP MAY BE BEST

You see the advertisements in newspapers, on TV, and on the Internet. You hear them on the radio. You get fliers in the mail. You may even get calls from telemarketers offering credit repair services. They all make the same claims:

- "Credit problems? No problem!"

- "We can erase your bad credit—100% guaranteed."

- "Create a new credit identity—legally."

- "We can remove bankruptcies, judgments, liens, and bad loans from your credit file forever!"

Do yourself a favor and save some money, too. Don't believe these statements. Only time, a conscious effort, and a personal debt repayment plan will improve your credit report. This brochure explains how you can improve your creditworthiness and gives legitimate resources for low or no-cost help.

THE SCAM

Every day, companies nationwide appeal to consumers with poor credit histories. They promise, for a fee, to clean up your credit report so you can get a car loan, a home mortgage, insurance, or even a job. The truth is, they can't deliver. After you pay them

Annual Credit Report Request Form

You have the right to get a free copy of your credit file disclosure, commonly called a credit report, once every 12 months, from each of the nationwide consumer credit reporting companies, Equifax, Experian and TransUnion.

For instant access to your free credit report, visit www.annualcreditreport.com.

For more information on obtaining your free credit report, visit www.annualcreditreport.com or call 877-322-8228

Use this form if you prefer to write to request your credit report from any, or all, of the nationwide consumer credit reporting companies. The following information is required to process your request. **Omission of any information may delay your request.**

Once complete, fold (do not staple or tape), place into a #10 envelope, affix required postage and mail to:
Annual Credit Report Request Service P.O. Box 105281 Atlanta, GA 30348-5281.

Please use a Black or Blue Pen and write your responses in PRINTED CAPITAL LETTERS without touching the sides of the boxes like the examples listed below:

A B C D E F G H I J K L M N O P Q R S T U V W X Y Z   0 1 2 3 4 5 6 7 8 9

Social Security Number:

Date of Birth:

Month   Day   Year

Fold Here   Fold Here

First Name   M.I.

Last Name   JR, SR, III, etc.

Current Mailing Address:

House Number   Street Name

Apartment Number / Private Mailbox   For Puerto Rico Only: Print Urbanization Name

City   State   ZipCode

Previous Mailing Address (complete only if at current mailing address for less than two years):

House Number   Street Name

Fold Here   Fold Here

Apartment Number / Private Mailbox   For Puerto Rico Only: Print Urbanization Name

City   State   ZipCode

Shade Circle Like This → ●

Not Like This → ⊗ ∅

I want a credit report from (shade each that you would like to receive):

○ Equifax
○ Experian
○ TransUnion

○ Shade here if, for security reasons, you want your credit report to include no more than the last four digits of your Social Security Number.

If additional information is needed to process your request, the consumer credit reporting company will contact you by mail.

Your request will be processed within 15 days of receipt and then mailed to you.

31238

Copyright 2004, Central Source LLC

hundreds or thousands of dollars in fees, these companies do nothing to improve your credit report; most simply vanish with your money.

THE WARNING SIGNS

If you decide to respond to a credit repair offer, look for these tell-tale signs of a scam:

- companies that want you to pay for credit repair services before they provide any services.

- companies that do not tell you your legal rights and what you can do for yourself for free.

- companies that recommend that you not contact a credit reporting company directly.

- companies that suggest that you try to invent a "new" credit identity—and then, a new credit report—by applying for an Employer Identification Number to use instead of your Social Security number.

- companies that advise you to dispute all information in your credit report or take any action that seems illegal, like creating a new credit identity. If you follow illegal advice and commit fraud, you may be subject to prosecution.

You could be charged and prosecuted for mail or wire fraud if you use the mail or telephone to apply for credit and provide false information. It's a federal crime to lie on a loan or credit application, to misrepresent your Social Security number, and to obtain an Employer Identification Number from the Internal Revenue Service under false pretenses. Under the Credit Repair Organizations Act, credit repair companies cannot require you to pay until they have completed the services they have promised.

THE TRUTH

No one can legally remove accurate and timely negative information from a credit report. The law allows you to ask for an investigation of information in your file that you dispute as inaccurate or incomplete. There is no charge for this. Everything a credit repair clinic can do for you legally, you can do for yourself at little or no cost. According to the Fair Credit Reporting Act (FCRA):

- You're entitled to a free report if a company takes adverse action against you, like denying your application for credit, insurance, or employment, and you ask for your report within

60 days of receiving notice of the action. The notice will give you the name, address, and phone number of the consumer reporting company. You're also entitled to one free report a year if you're unemployed and plan to look for a job within 60 days; if you're on welfare; or if your report is inaccurate because of fraud, including identity theft.

- Each of the nationwide consumer reporting companies—Equifax, Experian, and TransUnion—is required to provide you with a free copy of your credit report, at your request, once every 12 months. The three companies have set up a central website, a toll-free telephone number, and a mailing address through which you can order your free annual report. To order, click on annualcreditreport.com, call 1-877-322-8228, or complete the Annual Credit Report Request Form and mail it to: Annual Credit Report Request Service, P.O. Box 105281, Atlanta, GA 30348-5281. You can print the form from ftc.gov/credit. Do not contact the three nationwide consumer reporting companies individually. They are providing free annual credit reports only through annualcreditreport.com, 1-877-322-8228, and Annual Credit Report Request Service, P.O. Box 105281, Atlanta, GA 30348-5281. You may order your reports from each of the three nationwide consumer reporting companies at the same time, or you can order your report from each of the companies one at a time. For more information, see Your Access to Free Credit Reports at ftc.gov/credit. Otherwise, a consumer reporting company may charge you up to $9.50 for another copy of your report within a 12-month period.

- You can dispute mistakes or outdated items for free. Under the FCRA, both the consumer reporting company and the information provider (that is, the person, company, or organization that provides information about you to a consumer reporting company) are responsible for correcting inaccurate or incomplete information in your report. To take advantage of all your rights under this law, contact the consumer reporting company and the information provider.

STEP ONE

Tell the consumer reporting company, in writing, what information you think is inaccurate. Include copies (NOT originals) of documents that support your position. In addition to providing your complete name and address, your letter should clearly identify each item in your report you dispute, state the facts and explain why you dispute the information, and request that it be removed or corrected. You may want to enclose a copy of your report with the items in question circled. Your letter may look something like the one shown below. Send your letter by certified mail, "return receipt requested," so you can document what the consumer reporting company received. Keep copies of your dispute letter and enclosures.

Consumer reporting companies must investigate the items in question—usually within 30 days—unless they consider your dispute frivolous. They also must forward all the relevant data you provide about the inaccuracy to the organization that provided the information. After the information provider receives notice of a dispute from the consumer reporting company, it must investigate, review the relevant information, and report the results back to the consumer reporting company. If the information provider finds the disputed information is inaccurate, it must notify all three nationwide consumer reporting companies so they can correct the information in your file.

When the investigation is complete, the consumer reporting company must give you the results in writing and a free copy of your report if the dispute results in a change. If an item is changed or deleted, the consumer reporting company cannot put the disputed information back in your file unless the information provider verifies that it is accurate and complete. The consumer reporting company also must send you written notice that includes the name, address, and phone number of the information provider. If you request, the consumer reporting company must send notices of any correction to anyone who received your report in the past six months. You can have a corrected copy of your report sent to anyone who received a copy during the past two years for employment purposes.

If an investigation doesn't resolve your dispute with the consumer reporting company, you can ask that a statement of the dispute be included in your file and in future reports. You also can ask the consumer reporting company to provide your statement to anyone who received a copy of your report in the recent past. You can expect to pay a fee for this service.

STEP TWO

Tell the creditor or other information provider, in writing, that you dispute an item. Be sure to include copies (NOT originals) of documents that support your position. Many providers specify an address for disputes. If the provider reports the item to a consumer reporting company, it must include a notice of your dispute. And if you are correct—that is, if the information is found to be inaccurate—the information provider may not report it again.

For more information, see How to Dispute Credit Report Errors at ftc.gov/credit.

REPORTING ACCURATE NEGATIVE INFORMATION

When negative information in your report is accurate, only the passage of time can assure its removal. A consumer reporting company can report most accurate negative information for seven years and bankruptcy information for 10 years. Information about an unpaid judgment against you can be reported for seven years or until the statute of limitations runs out, whichever is longer. There is no time limit on reporting: information about criminal convictions; information reported in response to your application for a job that pays more than $75,000 a year; and information reported because you've applied for more than $150,000 worth of credit or life insurance. There is a standard method for calculating the seven-year reporting period. Generally, the period runs from the date that the event took place.

For more information, see Building a Better Credit Report at ftc.gov/credit.

THE CREDIT REPAIR ORGANIZATIONS ACT

By law, credit repair organizations must give you a copy of the "Consumer Credit File Rights Under State and Federal Law" before you sign a contract. They also must give you a written contract that spells out your rights and obligations. Read these documents before you sign anything. The law contains specific protections for you. For example, a credit repair company cannot:

- make false claims about their services

- charge you until they have completed the promised services

- perform any services until they have your signature on a written contract and have completed a three-day waiting period. During this time, you can cancel the contract without paying any fees

Your contract must specify:

- the payment terms for services, including their total cost

- a detailed description of the services to be performed

- how long it will take to achieve the results

- any guarantees they offer

- the company's name and business address

HAVE YOU BEEN VICTIMIZED?

Many states have laws regulating credit repair companies. State law enforcement officials may be helpful if you've lost money to credit repair scams.

If you've had a problem with a credit repair company, don't be embarrassed to report it. While you may fear that contacting the government will only make your problems worse, remember that laws are in place to protect you. Contact your local consumer affairs office or your state Attorney General (AGs). Many AGs have toll-free consumer hotlines. Check the Blue Pages of your telephone directory for the phone number or check www.naag.org for a list of state Attorneys General.

NEED HELP? DON'T DESPAIR

Just because you have a poor credit report doesn't mean you won't be able to get credit. Creditors set their own credit-granting standards and not all of them look at your credit history the same way. Some may look only at more recent years to evaluate you for credit, and they may grant credit if your bill-paying history has improved. It may be worthwhile to contact creditors informally to discuss their credit standards.

If you're not disciplined enough to create a workable budget and stick to it, work out a repayment plan with your creditors, or keep track of mounting bills, consider contacting a credit counseling organization. Many credit counseling organizations are nonprofit and work with you to solve your financial problems. But not all are reputable. For example, just because an organization says it's "nonprofit," there's no guarantee that its services are free, affordable, or even legitimate. In fact, some credit counseling organizations charge high fees, or hide their fees by pressuring consumers to make "voluntary" contributions that only cause more debt.

Most credit counselors offer services through local offices, the Internet, or on the telephone. If possible, find an organization that offers in-person counseling. Many universities, military bases, credit unions, housing authorities, and branches of the U.S. Cooperative Extension Service operate nonprofit credit counseling programs. Your financial institution, local consumer protection agency, and friends and family also may be good sources of information and referrals.

If you are considering filing for bankruptcy, you should know about one major change to the bankruptcy laws: As of October 17, 2005, you must get credit counseling from a government-approved organization within six months before you file for bankruptcy relief. You can find a state-by-state list of government-approved organizations at www.usdoj.gov/ust. That is the website of the U.S. Trustee Program, the organization within the U.S. Department of Justice that supervises bankruptcy cases and trustees.

Reputable credit counseling organizations can advise you on managing your money and debts, help you develop a budget, and offer free educational materials and workshops. Their counselors are certified and trained in the areas of consumer credit, money and debt management, and budgeting. Counselors discuss your entire financial situation with you, and help you develop a personalized plan to solve your money problems. An initial counseling session typically lasts an hour, with an offer of follow-up sessions. For more information, see Knee Deep in Debt and Fiscal Fitness: Choosing a Credit Counselor at ftc.gov/credit.

DO-IT-YOURSELF CHECK-UP

Even if you don't have a poor credit history, some financial advisors and consumer advocates suggest you review your credit report periodically

- because the information it contains affects whether you can get a loan or insurance—and how much you will have to pay for it.

- to make sure the information is accurate, complete, and up-to-date before you apply for a loan for a major purchase like a house or car, buy insurance, or apply for a job.

- to help guard against identity theft. That's when someone uses your personal information—like your name, your Social Security number, or your credit card number—to commit fraud. Identity thieves may use your information to open a new credit card account in your name. Then, when they don't pay the bills, the delinquent account is reported on your credit report. Inaccurate information like that could affect your ability to get credit, insurance, or even a job.

SAMPLE DISPUTE LETTER

Date

Your Name
Your Address
Your City, State, Zip Code

Complaint Department
Name of Company
Address
City, State, Zip Code

Dear Sir or Madam:

I am writing to dispute the following information in my file. The items I dispute also are encircled on the attached copy of the report I received.

This item (identify item(s) disputed by name of source, such as creditors or tax court, and identify type of item, such as credit account, judgment, etc.) is (inaccurate or incomplete) because (describe what is inaccurate or incomplete and why). I am requesting that the item be deleted (or request another specific change) to correct the information.

Enclosed are copies of (use this sentence if applicable and describe any enclosed documentation, such as payment records, court documents) supporting my position. Please investigate this (these) matter(s) and (delete or correct) the disputed item(s) as soon as possible.

Sincerely,
Your name

Enclosures *(list what you are enclosing)*

The FTC works for the consumer to prevent fraudulent, deceptive, and unfair business practices in the marketplace and to provide information to help consumers spot, stop, and avoid them. To file a complaint or to get free information on consumer issues, visit ftc.gov or call toll-free, 1-877-FTC-HELP (1-877-382-4357); TTY: 1-866-653-4261. The FTC enters consumer complaints into the Consumer Sentinel Network, a secure online database and investigative tool used by hundreds of civil and criminal law enforcement agencies in the U.S. and abroad.

Chapter Notes

1. From a brochure on the Federal Trade Commission website at: http://www.ftc.gov/bcp/conline/pubs/credit/repair.shtm.

B

Federal Programs

Fannie Mae

Fannie Mae[1] is a congressionally chartered corporation that buys mortgages on the secondary market[2], pools them and sells them as mortgage-backed securities[3] to investors on the open market.

The Federal Government established Fannie Mae in 1938 to keep the nation's mortgage money flowing by creating a secondary market. Fannie Mae was to serve as a refinance facility for federally insured mortgages that would help replenish the nation's supply of money.

In 1968, Fannie Mae became a private shareholder-owned company that works to make sure mortgage money is available for people in communities all across America. The organization does not lend money directly to homebuyers. Instead, Fannie Mae works with lenders to make sure they don't run out of mortgage funds, so more people can achieve the dream of homeownership.

Freddie Mac

In 1970 Congress chartered Freddie Mac[4], a stockholder-owned corporation, to create a never-ending flow of funds to mortgage lenders in support of homeownership and rental housing. Freddie Mac purchases mortgages from lenders, packages them into securities, and then sells them to investors. The goal is to help homeowners and renters enjoy lower housing costs and have better access to home financing.

The business strategies of these two companies differ, but both Fannie Mae and Freddie Mac have the same charter:

Fannie Mae's mission is "to help more families achieve the American Dream of homeownership by providing financial products and services that make it possible for low-, moderate-, and middle-income families to buy homes of their own."

Freddie Mac "ultimately provides low- to middle-income homeowners and renters with lower housing costs and better access to home financing."

National Housing Act

In 1934, Congress created the under the National Housing Act. The mission of the FHA was to contribute to the building and maintenance of healthy neighborhoods and to expand the opportunity of homeownership, rental housing and healthcare.

In 1965, the FHA was consolidated into the Department of Housing and Urban Development (HUD) Office of Housing with its mission: "to increase homeownership, support community development, and increase access to affordable housing free from discrimination."

Thanks to HUD's programs, Americans have more housing units available to them than anywhere else in the world.

Executive Order 5398, signed by President Herbert Hoover in 1930, created the Veterans Administration. In 1944, President

Franklin Roosevelt signed the "Servicemen's Readjustment Act of 1944" or more commonly known as "The GI Bill of Rights." This bill offered home loans and education benefits to veterans.

In 1989, the Department of Veterans Affairs (VA) was established, succeeding the Veterans Administration to become the 14th Department in the President's Cabinet.

The VA Home Loan Program guarantees loans that are made by private lenders, such as banks, savings & loans, or mortgage companies. To get a loan, a veteran must apply to a lender. If the loan is approved, the VA will guarantee a portion of it to the lender. This guaranty protects the lender against loss up to the amount guaranteed and allows a veteran to obtain favorable financing terms.

The VA does not have a maximum loan amount, but lenders generally limit VA loans to $625,000[5] with no down payment (if income and credit qualifies). With a down payment, loans can exceed $625,000.

Veterans do not have to be first time homebuyers to use this loan program and may reuse his/her benefit.[6]

Ginnie Mae

The Housing and Urban Development Act established Ginnie Mae[7] in 1968 as a wholly owned corporation within HUD. Its purpose was—and still is—to serve as a secondary mortgage market institution for low and moderate-income FHA, VA (Veteran Administration), and RHS (Rural Housing Service) homebuyers.

The Rural Housing Service (RHS) was created in 1994 to meet the housing and community development needs of rural America and is an agency within the Department of Agriculture.

More rural families and individuals may be able to become homeowners with the help of RHS programs. RHS programs are available to help low- to moderate-income rural residents to purchase, construct, repair, or relocate a dwelling and related facilities. U.S. Department of Agriculture rural housing loan programs allow qualified homebuyers to get loans with minimal closing costs and no down payment.

Single Family Housing

Direct Loan Program[8]—Individuals or families receive financial assistance directly from the Rural Housing Service in the form of a home loan at an affordable interest rate. Most loans made under the Direct Loan Program are to families with income below 80% of the median income level in the communities where they live.

Because RHS is able to make loans to those who will not qualify for a conventional loan, the RHS Direct Loan program enables more people to buy homes than might otherwise be possible. Direct loans may be made for the purchase of an existing home or for new home construction.

Loan Guarantee Program[9]—Under the Guaranteed Loan program, the Rural Housing Service guarantees loans made by private sector lenders. A loan guarantee through RHS means that, should the borrower default on the loan, RHS will pay the private financier for the loan. The borrower works with the private lender and makes his or her payments to that lender.

Under the terms of the program, an individual or family may borrow up to 100% of the appraised value of the home, which eliminates the need for a down payment. Because a common barrier to owning a home for many low-income homebuyers is the lack of funds to make a down payment, the availability of loan guarantees from RHS makes owning a home available to a larger percentage of Americans.

Mutual Self-Help Housing Program[10]—The Mutual Self-Help Housing Program makes homes affordable by enabling future home-owners to work on homes themselves. With this investment in the home, or "sweat equity", each homeowner pays less for his or her home. Each qualified applicant is required to complete 65% of the work to build his or her own home.

Technical Assistance Grants and Site Loans are provided to non-profit and local government organizations, which supervise groups of 5 to 12 enrollees in the Self-Help Program. Members of each group help work on each other's homes, moving in only when all the homes are completed.

Once accepted into the Self-Help Housing Program, each individual enrollee generally applies for a Single-Family Housing Direct Loan (Section 502).

For a list of Guaranteed Loan Income Limits[11] for individuals wanting to purchase rural single family homes across the United States, visit the RHS Single Family Housing Guaranteed Loan Income Limits website.

Homes for Sale[12]—The Single Family Housing "Real Estate for Sale" web site provides an online guide to Government owned real estate and potential foreclosure sales information on single-family homes. The site provides access to detailed information about each of the properties and links to other USDA web sites providing a variety of services.

Chapter Notes

1. www.fanniemae.com

2. Secondary market: A market in which existing mortgages and mortgage-backed securities are traded.

3. Mortgage-backed security (MBS): Security backed by a pool of mortgages, such as those issued by Ginnie Mae and Freddie Mac. Also called mortgage-backed certificate.

4. www.freddiemac.com

5. as of September 2008

6. www.rurdev.usda.gov/rhs/

7. www.GinnieMae.gov

8. www.rurdev.usda.gov/rhs/sfh/brief_rhdirect.htm

9. www.rurdev.usda.gov/rhs/sfh/brief_rhguar.htm

10. www.rurdev.usda.gov/rhs/sfh/brief_selfhelpsite.htm

11. http://www.rurdev.usda.gov/rhs/sfh/sfh%20guaranteed%20loan%20income%20limits.htm

12. http://www.resales.usda.gov/

Good Faith Estimate Settlement Statement

You must receive a "Truth-in-Lending" (TIL) statement and a "good faith estimate" (GFE) from your prospective lender within three days of signing your real estate mortgage loan application. The TIL statement must include a disclosure of the Annual Percentage Rate (APR) you will pay. The good faith estimate shows all the costs you will be required to pay at closing; it is not a guarantee of all your costs or of the total due at closing. Read it carefully and have it with you at closing.

The Settlement Statement, or HUD-1 as it is sometimes called, is required by federal law and must be presented to you no later than at closing. It itemizes all the services provided in connection with the mortgage loan and lists all the charges to the buyer and seller. It is to your benefit to obtain the Settlement Statement 24 hours before closing so you have time to review and compare the charges shown with those on the good faith estimate you received when you applied for your loan.

The HUD-1 form is reproduced in this section of the appendix.

OMB Approval No. 2502-0265

Good Faith Estimate (GFE)

Name of Originator		Borrower	
Originator Address		Property Address	
Originator Phone Number			
Originator Email		Date of GFE	

Purpose

This GFE gives you an estimate of your settlement charges and loan terms if you are approved for this loan. For more information, see HUD's *Special Information Booklet* on settlement charges, your *Truth-in-Lending Disclosures*, and other consumer information at www.hud.gov/respa. If you decide you would like to proceed with this loan, contact us.

Shopping for your loan

Only you can shop for the best loan for you. Compare this GFE with other loan offers, so you can find the best loan. Use the shopping chart on page 3 to compare all the offers you receive.

Important dates

1. The interest rate for this GFE is available through [   ]. After this time, the interest rate, some of your loan Origination Charges, and the monthly payment shown below can change until you lock your interest rate.

2. This estimate for all other settlement charges is available through [   ]

3. After you lock your interest rate, you must go to settlement within [ ] days (your rate lock period) to receive the locked interest rate.

4. You must lock the interest rate at least [ ] days before settlement.

Summary of your loan

Your initial loan amount is	$
Your loan term is	years
Your initial interest rate is	%
Your initial monthly amount owed for principal, interest, and any mortgage insurance is	$ per month
Can your interest rate rise?	☐ No ☐ Yes, it can rise to a maximum of %. The first change will be in
Even if you make payments on time, can your loan balance rise?	☐ No ☐ Yes, it can rise to a maximum of $
Even if you make payments on time, can your monthly amount owed for principal, interest, and any mortgage insurance rise?	☐ No ☐ Yes, the first increase can be in and the monthly amount owed can rise to $ The maximum it can ever rise to is $
Does your loan have a prepayment penalty?	☐ No ☐ Yes, your maximum prepayment penalty is $
Does your loan have a balloon payment?	☐ No ☐ Yes, you have a balloon payment of $ due in years

Escrow account information

Some lenders require an escrow account to hold funds for paying property taxes or other property-related charges in addition to your monthly amount owed of $[   ].
Do we require you to have an escrow account for your loan?
☐ No, you do not have an escrow account. You must pay these charges directly when due.
☐ Yes, you have an escrow account. It may or may not cover all of these charges. Ask us.

Summary of your settlement charges

A	Your Adjusted Origination Charges *(See page 2)*	$
B	Your Charges for All Other Settlement Services *(See page 2)*	$
A + B	Total Estimated Settlement Charges	$

Understanding
your estimated
settlement charges

Your Adjusted Origination Charges

1. Our origination charge
   This charge is for getting this loan for you.

2. Your credit or charge (points) for the specific interest rate chosen
   - ☐ The credit or charge for the interest rate of [____] % is included in "Our origination charge." (See item 1 above.)
   - ☐ You receive a credit of $ [_____] for this interest rate of [____] %. This credit **reduces** your settlement charges.
   - ☐ You pay a charge of $ [_____] for this interest rate of [____] %. This charge (points) **increases** your total settlement charges.

   The tradeoff table on page 3 shows that you can change your total settlement charges by choosing a different interest rate for this loan.

A | Your Adjusted Origination Charges | $

Your Charges for All Other Settlement Services

Some of these charges can change at settlement. See the top of page 3 for more information.

3. Required services that we select
   These charges are for services we require to complete your settlement. We will choose the providers of these services.

Service	Charge

4. Title services and lender's title insurance
   This charge includes the services of a title or settlement agent, for example, and title insurance to protect the lender, if required.

5. Owner's title insurance
   You may purchase an owner's title insurance policy to protect your interest in the property.

6. Required services that you can shop for
   These charges are for other services that are required to complete your settlement. We can identify providers of these services or you can shop for them yourself. Our estimates for providing these services are below.

Service	Charge

7. Government recording charges
   These charges are for state and local fees to record your loan and title documents.

8. Transfer taxes
   These charges are for state and local fees on mortgages and home sales.

9. Initial deposit for your escrow account
   This charge is held in an escrow account to pay future recurring charges on your property and includes ☐ all property taxes, ☐ all insurance, and ☐ other [_____]

10. Daily interest charges
    This charge is for the daily interest on your loan from the day of your settlement until the first day of the next month or the first day of your normal mortgage payment cycle. This amount is $ [____] per day for [____] days (if your settlement is [_____]).

11. Homeowner's insurance
    This charge is for the insurance you must buy for the property to protect from a loss, such as fire.

Policy	Charge

B | Your Charges for All Other Settlement Services | $

A + **B** | Total Estimated Settlement Charges | $

 Good Faith Estimate (HUD-GFE) 2

Instructions

Understanding which charges can change at settlement

This GFE estimates your settlement charges. At your settlement, you will receive a HUD-1, a form that lists your actual costs. Compare the charges on the HUD-1 with the charges on this GFE. Charges can change if you select your own provider and do not use the companies we identify. (See below for details.)

These charges **cannot increase** at settlement:	The total of these charges **can increase up to 10%** at settlement:	These charges **can change** at settlement:
• Our origination charge • Your credit or charge (points) for the specific interest rate chosen *(after you lock in your interest rate)* • Your adjusted origination charges *(after you lock in your interest rate)* • Transfer taxes	• Required services that we select • Title services and lender's title insurance *(if we select them or you use companies we identify)* • Owner's title insurance *(if you use companies we identify)* • Required services that you can shop for *(if you use companies we identify)* • Government recording charges	• Required services that you can shop for *(if you do not use companies we identify)* • Title services and lender's title insurance *(if you do not use companies we identify)* • Owner's title insurance *(if you do not use companies we identify)* • Initial deposit for your escrow account • Daily interest charges • Homeowner's insurance

Using the tradeoff table

In this GFE, we offered you this loan with a particular interest rate and estimated settlement charges. However:

- If you want to choose this same loan with **lower settlement charges**, then you will have a **higher interest rate**.
- If you want to choose this same loan with a **lower interest rate**, then you will have **higher settlement charges**.

If you would like to choose an available option, you must ask us for a new GFE.

Loan originators have the option to complete this table. Please ask for additional information if the table is not completed.

	The loan in this GFE	The same loan with lower settlement charges	The same loan with a lower interest rate
Your initial loan amount	$	$	$
Your initial interest rate†	%	%	%
Your initial monthly amount owed	$	$	$
Change in the monthly amount owed from this GFE	No change	You will pay $ **more** every month	You will pay $ **less** every month
Change in the amount you will pay at settlement with this interest rate	No change	Your settlement charges will be **reduced** by $	Your settlement charges will **increase** by $
How much your total estimated settlement charges will be	$	$	$

† *For an adjustable rate loan, the comparisons above are for the initial interest rate before adjustments are made.*

Using the shopping chart

Use this chart to compare GFEs from different loan originators. Fill in the information by using a different column for each GFE you receive. By comparing loan offers, you can shop for the best loan.

	This loan	Loan 2	Loan 3	Loan 4
Loan originator name				
Initial loan amount				
Loan term				
Initial interest rate				
Initial monthly amount owed				
Rate lock period				
Can interest rate rise?				
Can loan balance rise?				
Can monthly amount owed rise?				
Prepayment penalty?				
Balloon payment?				
Total Estimated Settlement Charges				

If your loan is sold in the future

Some lenders may sell your loan after settlement. Any fees lenders receive in the future cannot change the loan you receive or the charges you paid at settlement.

 Good Faith Estimate (HUD-GFE) 3

OMB Approval No. 2502-0265

 A. **Settlement Statement (HUD-1)**

B. Type of Loan

1. ☐ FHA	2. ☐ RHS	3. ☐ Conv. Unins.	6. File Number:	7. Loan Number:	8. Mortgage Insurance Case Number:
4. ☐ VA	5. ☐ Conv. Ins.				

C. Note: This form is furnished to give you a statement of actual settlement costs. Amounts paid to and by the settlement agent are shown. Items marked "(p.o.c.)" were paid outside the closing; they are shown here for informational purposes and are not included in the totals.

D. Name & Address of Borrower:	E. Name & Address of Seller:	F. Name & Address of Lender:
G. Property Location:	H. Settlement Agent:	I. Settlement Date:
	Place of Settlement:	

J. Summary of Borrower's Transaction		K. Summary of Seller's Transaction	
100. Gross Amount Due from Borrower		**400. Gross Amount Due to Seller**	
101. Contract sales price		401. Contract sales price	
102. Personal property		402. Personal property	
103. Settlement charges to borrower (line 1400)		403.	
104.		404.	
105.		405.	
Adjustment for items paid by seller in advance		Adjustment for items paid by seller in advance	
106. City/town taxes to		406. City/town taxes to	
107. County taxes to		407. County taxes to	
108. Assessments to		408. Assessments to	
109.		409.	
110.		410.	
111.		411.	
112.		412.	
120. Gross Amount Due from Borrower		**420. Gross Amount Due to Seller**	
200. Amount Paid by or in Behalf of Borrower		**500. Reductions In Amount Due to seller**	
201. Deposit or earnest money		501. Excess deposit (see instructions)	
202. Principal amount of new loan(s)		502. Settlement charges to seller (line 1400)	
203. Existing loan(s) taken subject to		503. Existing loan(s) taken subject to	
204.		504. Payoff of first mortgage loan	
205.		505. Payoff of second mortgage loan	
206.		506.	
207.		507.	
208.		508.	
209.		509.	
Adjustments for items unpaid by seller		Adjustments for items unpaid by seller	
210. City/town taxes to		510. City/town taxes to	
211. County taxes to		511. County taxes to	
212. Assessments to		512. Assessments to	
213.		513.	
214.		514.	
215.		515.	
216.		516.	
217.		517.	
218.		518.	
219.		519.	
220. Total Paid by/for Borrower		**520. Total Reduction Amount Due Seller**	
300. Cash at Settlement from/to Borrower		**600. Cash at Settlement to/from Seller**	
301. Gross amount due from borrower (line 120)		601. Gross amount due to seller (line 420)	
302. Less amounts paid by/for borrower (line 220)	( )	602. Less reductions in amounts due seller (line 520)	( )
303. Cash ☐ From ☐ To Borrower		**603. Cash** ☐ To ☐ From Seller	

The Public Reporting Burden for this collection of information is estimated at 35 minutes per response for collecting, reviewing, and reporting the data. This agency may not collect this information, and you are not required to complete this form, unless it displays a currently valid OMB control number. No confidentiality is assured; this disclosure is mandatory. This is designed to provide the parties to a RESPA covered transaction with information during the settlement process.

L. Settlement Charges

700. Total Real Estate Broker Fees

	Paid From Borrower's Funds at Settlement	Paid From Seller's Funds at Settlement
Division of commission (line 700) as follows :		
701. $ to		
702. $ to		
703. Commission paid at settlement		
704.		

800. Items Payable in Connection with Loan

				Paid From Borrower's Funds at Settlement	Paid From Seller's Funds at Settlement
801. Our origination charge		$	(from GFE #1)		
802. Your credit or charge (points) for the specific interest rate chosen		$	(from GFE #2)		
803. Your adjusted origination charges			(from GFE #A)		
804. Appraisal fee to			(from GFE #3)		
805. Credit report to			(from GFE #3)		
806. Tax service to			(from GFE #3)		
807. Flood certification to			(from GFE #3)		
808.					
809.					
810.					
811.					

900. Items Required by Lender to be Paid in Advance

					Paid From Borrower's Funds at Settlement	Paid From Seller's Funds at Settlement
901. Daily interest charges from	to	@ $	/day	(from GFE #10)		
902. Mortgage insurance premium for	months to			(from GFE #3)		
903. Homeowner's insurance for	years to			(from GFE #11)		
904.						

1000. Reserves Deposited with Lender

				Paid From Borrower's Funds at Settlement	Paid From Seller's Funds at Settlement
1001. Initial deposit for your escrow account			(from GFE #9)		
1002. Homeowner's insurance	months @ $	per month $			
1003. Mortgage insurance	months @ $	per month $			
1004. Property Taxes	months @ $	per month $			
1005.	months @ $	per month $			
1006.	months @ $	per month $			
1007. Aggregate Adjustment		-$			

1100. Title Charges

			Paid From Borrower's Funds at Settlement	Paid From Seller's Funds at Settlement
1101. Title services and lender's title insurance		(from GFE #4)		
1102. Settlement or closing fee	$			
1103. Owner's title insurance		(from GFE #5)		
1104. Lender's title insurance	$			
1105. Lender's title policy limit $				
1106. Owner's title policy limit $				
1107. Agent's portion of the total title insurance premium to	$			
1108. Underwriter's portion of the total title insurance premium to	$			
1109.				
1110.				
1111.				

1200. Government Recording and Transfer Charges

				Paid From Borrower's Funds at Settlement	Paid From Seller's Funds at Settlement
1201. Government recording charges			(from GFE #7)		
1202. Deed $	Mortgage $	Release $			
1203. Transfer taxes			(from GFE #8)		
1204. City/County tax/stamps	Deed $	Mortgage $			
1205. State tax/stamps	Deed $	Mortgage $			
1206.					

1300. Additional Settlement Charges

			Paid From Borrower's Funds at Settlement	Paid From Seller's Funds at Settlement
1301. Required services that you can shop for		(from GFE #6)		
1302.	$			
1303.	$			
1304.				
1305.				

1400. Total Settlement Charges (enter on lines 103, Section J and 502, Section K)

	Paid From Borrower's Funds at Settlement	Paid From Seller's Funds at Settlement

Comparison of Good Faith Estimate (GFE) and HUD-1 Charrges		Good Faith Estimate	HUD-1
Charges That Cannot Increase	HUD-1 Line Number		
Our origination charge	# 801		
Your credit or charge (points) for the specific interest rate chosen	# 802		
Your adjusted origination charges	# 803		
Transfer taxes	# 1203		

Charges That In Total Cannot Increase More Than 10%		Good Faith Estimate	HUD-1
Government recording charges	# 1201		
	#		
	#		
	#		
	#		
	#		
	#		
	#		
	Total		
	Increase between GFE and HUD-1 Charges	$ or %	

Charges That Can Change		Good Faith Estimate	HUD-1
Initial deposit for your escrow account	# 1001		
Daily interest charges $ /day	# 901		
Homeowner's insurance	# 903		
	#		
	#		
	#		

Loan Terms

Your initial loan amount is	$
Your loan term is	years
Your initial interest rate is	%
Your initial monthly amount owed for principal, interest, and any mortgage insurance is	$ includes ☐ Principal ☐ Interest ☐ Mortgage Insurance
Can your interest rate rise?	☐ No ☐ Yes, it can rise to a maximum of %. The first change will be on and can change again every after . Every change date, your interest rate can increase or decrease by %. Over the life of the loan, your interest rate is guaranteed to never be **lower than** % or **higher than** %.
Even if you make payments on time, can your loan balance rise?	☐ No ☐ Yes, it can rise to a maximum of $
Even if you make payments on time, can your monthly amount owed for principal, interest, and mortgage insurance rise?	☐ No ☐ Yes, the first increase can be on and the monthly amount owed can rise to $. The maximum it can ever rise to is $.
Does your loan have a prepayment penalty?	☐ No ☐ Yes, your maximum prepayment penalty is $
Does your loan have a balloon payment?	☐ No ☐ Yes, you have a balloon payment of $ due in years on
Total monthly amount owed including escrow account payments	☐ You do not have a monthly escrow payment for items, such as property taxes and homeowner's insurance. You must pay these items directly yourself. ☐ You have an additional monthly escrow payment of $ that results in a total initial monthly amount owed of $. This includes principal, interest, any mortgage insurance and any items checked below: ☐ Property taxes ☐ Homeowner's insurance ☐ Flood insurance ☐ ☐

Note: If you have any questions about the Settlement Charges and Loan Terms listed on this form, please contact your lender.

D

Residential Sales Contract

D on't expect to see your local Board of REALTORS®contract accepted by all homebuilders when you are purchasing a home under construction or just completed. Usually, home builders will use their own sales contracts or purchase agreements.

While contracts to purchase residential real estate differ from state to state, here is a contract used in Illinois. In my opinion, it's an outstanding model which you can compare with a contract presented to you when you're buying your first home.

Courtesy of IRELA and the Chicago Board of REALTORS®

MULTI-BOARD RESIDENTIAL REAL ESTATE CONTRACT 5.0

1 **1. THE PARTIES:** Buyer and Seller are hereinafter referred to as the "Parties".

2 Buyer(s) (Please Print) _____

3 Seller(s) (Please Print) _____

4 **If Dual Agency applies, complete Optional Paragraph 41.**

5 **2. THE REAL ESTATE:** Real Estate shall be defined as the Property, all improvements, the fixtures and
6 Personal Property included therein. Seller agrees to convey to Buyer or to Buyer's designated grantee, the
7 Real Estate with the approximate lot size or acreage of _____ commonly known as:

8 _____
9 Address   City   State   Zip

10 _____
11 County   Unit # (if applicable)   Permanent Index Number(s) of Real Estate

12 **If Condo/Coop/Townhome Parking is Included**: # of space(s) ____ ; identified as Space(s) #_____ ;
13 *(check type)* ❏ deeded space ❏ limited common element ❏ assigned space.

14 **3. FIXTURES AND PERSONAL PROPERTY:** All of the fixtures and included Personal Property are owned by
15 Seller and to Seller's knowledge are in operating condition on the Date of Acceptance, unless otherwise
16 stated herein. Seller agrees to transfer to Buyer all fixtures, all heating, electrical, plumbing and well systems
17 together with the following items of Personal Property by Bill of Sale at Closing:
18 *[Check or enumerate applicable items]*

19 __ Refrigerator	__ Central Air Conditioning	__ Central Humidifier	__ Light Fixtures, as they exist
20 __ Oven/Range/Stove	__ Window Air Conditioners	__ Water Softener (owned)	__ Built-in or Attached Shelving
21 __ Microwave	__ Ceiling Fan(s)	__ Sump Pumps	__ All Window Treatments & Hardware
22 __ Dishwasher	__ Intercom System	__ Electronic or Media Air Filter	__ Existing Storms & Screens
23 __ Garbage Disposal	__ TV Antenna System	__ Central Vac & Equipment	__ Fireplace Screens/Doors/Grates
24 __ Trash Compactor	__ Satellite Dish	__ Security Systems (owned)	__ Fireplace Gas Logs
25 __ Washer	__ Outdoor Shed	__ Garage Door Openers	__ Invisible Fence System, Collars & Box
26 __ Dryer	__ Planted Vegetation	with all Transmitters	__ Smoke Detectors
27 __ Attached Gas Grill	__ Outdoor Playsets	__ All Tacked Down Carpeting	__ Carbon Monoxide Detectors

28 **Other items included:** _____
29 **Items NOT included:** _____
30 Seller warrants to Buyer that all fixtures, systems and Personal Property included in this Contract shall be in
31 operating condition at Possession, except: _____ .
32 A system or item shall be deemed to be in operating condition if it performs the function for which it is
33 intended, regardless of age, and does not constitute a threat to health or safety.
34 **Home Warranty ❏ shall ❏ shall not be included at a Premium not to exceed $_____ .**

35 **4. PURCHASE PRICE:** Purchase Price of $_____ shall be paid as follows: Initial earnest money
36 of $_____ by ❏ check, ❏ cash **OR** ❏ note due on _____ , 20___ to be increased
37 to a total of $_____ by _____ , 20___. The earnest money shall be held by the
38 *[check one]* ❏ Seller's Broker ❏ Buyer's Broker as "Escrowee", in trust for the mutual benefit of the Parties.
39 The balance of the Purchase Price, as adjusted by prorations, shall be paid at Closing by wire transfer of

Buyer Initial _____	*Buyer Initial* _____	*Seller Initial* _____	*Seller Initial* _____
Address _____			v5.0e

1

40 funds, or by certified, cashier's, mortgage lender's or title company's check (provided that the title company's
41 check is guaranteed by a licensed title insurance company).

42 **5. CLOSING:** Closing or escrow payout shall be on _____, 20____ or at such time as mutually
43 agreed by the Parties in writing. Closing shall take place at the escrow office of the title company (or its
44 issuing agent) that will issue the Owner's Policy of Title Insurance, situated nearest the Real Estate or as shall
45 be agreed mutually by the Parties.

46 **6. POSSESSION:** Unless otherwise provided in Paragraph 39, Seller shall deliver possession to Buyer at the
47 time of Closing. Possession shall be deemed to have been delivered when Seller has vacated the Real Estate
48 and delivered keys to the Real Estate to Buyer or to the office of the Seller's Broker.

49 **7. STATUTORY DISCLOSURES:** If applicable, prior to signing this Contract, Buyer *[check one]* ❏ has ❏ has
50 not received a completed Illinois Residential Real Property Disclosure Report; *[check one]* ❏ has ❏ has not
51 received the EPA Pamphlet, "Protect Your Family From Lead in Your Home"; *[check one]* ❏ has ❏ has not
52 received a Lead-Based Paint Disclosure; *[check one]* ❏ has ❏ has not received the IEMA Pamphlet "Radon
53 Testing Guidelines for Real Estate Transactions"; *[check one]* ❏ has ❏ has not received the Disclosure of
54 Information on Radon Hazards.

55 **8. PRORATIONS:** Proratable items shall include, without limitation, rents and deposits (if any) from tenants;
56 Special Service Area or Special Assessment Area tax for the year of Closing only; utilities, water and sewer;
57 and Homeowner or Condominium Association fees (and Master/Umbrella Association fees, if applicable).
58 Accumulated reserves of a Homeowner/Condominium Association(s) are not a proratable item. Seller
59 represents that as of the Date of Acceptance Homeowner/Condominium Association(s) fees are $_____
60 per _____ (and, if applicable, Master/Umbrella Association fees are $_____ per _____). Seller agrees
61 to pay prior to or at Closing any special assessments (by any association or governmental entity) confirmed
62 prior to the Date of Acceptance. Installments due after the year of Closing for a Special Assessment Area or
63 Special Service Area shall not be a proratable item and shall be payable by Buyer. The general Real Estate
64 taxes shall be prorated as of the date of Closing based on _____% of the most recent ascertainable full year
65 tax bill. All prorations shall be final as of Closing, except as provided in Paragraph 20. If the amount of the
66 most recent ascertainable full year tax bill reflects a homeowner, senior citizen or other exemption, a senior
67 freeze or senior deferral, then Seller has submitted or will submit in a timely manner all necessary
68 documentation to the appropriate governmental entity, before or after Closing, to preserve said exemption(s).

69 **9. ATTORNEY REVIEW:** Within five (5) Business Days after the Date of Acceptance, the attorneys for the
70 respective Parties, by Notice, may:
71 (a) Approve this Contract; or
72 (b) Disapprove this Contract, which disapproval shall not be based solely upon the Purchase Price; or
73 (c) Propose modifications except for the Purchase Price. If within ten (10) Business Days after the Date of
74   Acceptance written agreement is not reached by the Parties with respect to resolution of the proposed
75   modifications, then either Party may terminate this Contract by serving Notice, whereupon this Contract
76   shall be null and void; or
77 (d) Propose suggested changes to this Contract. If such suggestions are not agreed upon, neither Party may
78   declare this Contract null and void and this Contract shall remain in full force and effect.
79 **Unless otherwise specified, all Notices shall be deemed made pursuant to Paragraph 9(c). If Notice is not
80 served within the time specified herein, the provisions of this paragraph shall be deemed waived by the
81 Parties and this Contract shall remain in full force and effect.**

Buyer Initial _____ *Buyer Initial* _____ *Seller Initial* _____ *Seller Initial* _____

Address _____ v5.0e

82 **10. PROFESSIONAL INSPECTIONS AND INSPECTION NOTICES:** Buyer may conduct at Buyer's expense
83 (unless otherwise provided by governmental regulations) a home, radon, environmental, lead-based paint
84 and/or lead-based paint hazards (unless separately waived), and/or wood destroying insect infestation
85 inspection of the Real Estate by one or more licensed or certified inspection service(s).
86 (a) Buyer agrees that minor repairs and routine maintenance items of the Real Estate do not constitute
87   defects and are not a part of this contingency. **The fact that a functioning major component may be at**
88   **the end of its useful life shall not render such component defective for purposes of this paragraph.**
89   Buyer shall indemnify Seller and hold Seller harmless from and against any loss or damage caused by the
90   acts or negligence of Buyer or any person performing any inspection. The home inspection shall cover
91   only the major components of the Real Estate, including but not limited to central heating system(s),
92   central cooling system(s), plumbing and well system, electrical system, roof, walls, windows, ceilings,
93   floors, appliances and foundation. A major component shall be deemed to be in operating condition if it
94   performs the function for which it is intended, regardless of age, and does not constitute a threat to health
95   or safety. If radon mitigation is performed, Seller shall pay for any retest.
96 (b) Buyer shall serve Notice upon Seller or Seller's attorney of any defects disclosed by any inspection for
97   which Buyer requests resolution by Seller, together with a copy of the pertinent pages of the inspection
98   reports within five (5) Business Days (ten (10) calendar days for a lead-based paint and/or lead-based
99   paint hazard inspection) after the Date of Acceptance. If within ten (10) Business Days after the Date of
100 Acceptance written agreement is not reached by the Parties with respect to resolution of all inspection
101 issues, then either Party may terminate this Contract by serving Notice to the other Party, whereupon this
102 Contract shall be null and void.
103 (c) Notwithstanding anything to the contrary set forth above in this paragraph, in the event the inspection
104 reveals that the condition of the Real Estate is unacceptable to Buyer and Buyer serves Notice to Seller
105 within five (5) Business Days after the Date of Acceptance, this Contract shall be null and void.
106 (d) Failure of Buyer to conduct said inspection(s) and notify Seller within the time specified operates as a
107 waiver of Buyer's right to terminate this Contract under this Paragraph 10 and this Contract shall remain
108 in full force and effect.

109 **11. MORTGAGE CONTINGENCY:** This Contract is contingent upon Buyer obtaining a firm written mortgage
110 commitment (except for matters of title and survey or matters totally within Buyer's control) on or before
111 _____, 20___ for a *[check one]* ❏ fixed ❏ adjustable; *[check one]* ❏ conventional ❏ FHA/VA
112 (if FHA/VA is chosen, complete Paragraph 35) ❏ other_____ loan of _____% of Purchase
113 Price, plus private mortgage insurance (PMI), if required. The interest rate (initial rate, if applicable) shall not
114 exceed _____% per annum, amortized over not less than _____ years. Buyer shall pay loan origination fee
115 and/or discount points not to exceed _____% of the loan amount. Buyer shall pay the cost of application,
116 usual and customary processing fees and closing costs charged by lender. (Complete Paragraph 33 if closing
117 cost credits apply.) Buyer shall make written loan application within five (5) Business Days after the Date of
118 Acceptance. **Failure to do so shall constitute an act of Default under this Contract. If Buyer, having applied**
119 **for the loan specified above, is unable to obtain such loan commitment and serves Notice to Seller within**
120 **the time specified, this Contract shall be null and void. If Notice of inability to obtain such loan**
121 **commitment is not served within the time specified, Buyer shall be deemed to have waived this**
122 **contingency and this Contract shall remain in full force and effect. Unless otherwise provided in**
123 **Paragraph 31, this Contract shall not be contingent upon the sale and/or closing of Buyer's existing real**
124 **estate.** Buyer shall be deemed to have satisfied the financing conditions of this paragraph if Buyer obtains a
125 loan commitment in accordance with the terms of this paragraph even though the loan is conditioned on the
126 sale and/or closing of Buyer's existing real estate. If Seller at Seller's option and expense, within thirty (30)
127 days after Buyer's Notice, procures for Buyer such commitment or notifies Buyer that Seller will accept a

Buyer Initial _____ _Buyer Initial_ _____ _Seller Initial_ _____ _Seller Initial_ _____

Address _____ v5.0e

128 purchase money mortgage upon the same terms, this Contract shall remain in full force and effect. In such
129 event, Seller shall notify Buyer within five (5) Business Days after Buyer's Notice of Seller's election to
130 provide or obtain such financing, and Buyer shall furnish to Seller or lender all requested information and
131 shall sign all papers necessary to obtain the mortgage commitment and to close the loan.

132 **12. HOMEOWNER INSURANCE:** This Contract is contingent upon Buyer obtaining evidence of insurability for
133 an Insurance Service Organization HO-3 or equivalent policy at standard premium rates within ten (10)
134 Business Days after the Date of Acceptance. **If Buyer is unable to obtain evidence of insurability and serves**
135 **Notice with proof of same to Seller within the time specified, this Contract shall be null and void. If**
136 **Notice is not served within the time specified, Buyer shall be deemed to have waived this contingency**
137 **and this Contract shall remain in full force and effect.**

138 **13. FLOOD INSURANCE:** Unless previously disclosed in the Illinois Residential Real Property Disclosure
139 Report, Buyer shall have the option to declare this Contract null and void if the Real Estate is located in a
140 special flood hazard area which requires Buyer to carry flood insurance. **If Notice of the option to declare**
141 **this Contract null and void is not given to Seller within ten (10) Business Days after the Date of**
142 **Acceptance or by the Mortgage Contingency deadline date described in Paragraph 11 (whichever is later),**
143 **Buyer shall be deemed to have waived such option and this Contract shall remain in full force and effect.**
144 Nothing herein shall be deemed to affect any rights afforded by the Residential Real Property Disclosure Act.

145 **14. CONDOMINIUM/COMMON INTEREST ASSOCIATIONS:** (If applicable) The Parties agree that the terms
146 contained in this paragraph, which may be contrary to other terms of this Contract, shall supersede any
147 conflicting terms.
148 (a) Title when conveyed shall be good and merchantable, subject to terms, provisions, covenants and
149   conditions of the Declaration of Condominium/Covenants, Conditions and Restrictions and all
150   amendments; public and utility easements including any easements established by or implied from the
151   Declaration of Condominium/Covenants, Conditions and Restrictions or amendments thereto; party wall
152   rights and agreements; limitations and conditions imposed by the Condominium Property Act;
153   installments due after the date of Closing of general assessments established pursuant to the Declaration
154   of Condominium/Covenants, Conditions and Restrictions.
155 (b) Seller shall be responsible for payment of all regular assessments due and levied prior to Closing and for
156   all special assessments confirmed prior to the Date of Acceptance.
157 (c) Buyer has, within five (5) Business Days from the Date of Acceptance, the right to demand from Seller
158   items as stipulated by the Illinois Condominium Property Act, if applicable, and Seller shall diligently
159   apply for same. This Contract is subject to the condition that Seller be able to procure and provide to
160   Buyer, a release or waiver of any option of first refusal or other pre-emptive rights of purchase created by
161   the Declaration of Condominium/Covenants, Conditions and Restrictions within the time established by
162   the Declaration of Condominium/Covenants, Conditions and Restrictions. In the event the
163   Condominium Association requires the personal appearance of Buyer and/or additional documentation,
164   Buyer agrees to comply with same.
165 (d) In the event the documents and information provided by Seller to Buyer disclose that the existing
166   improvements are in violation of existing rules, regulations or other restrictions or that the terms and
167   conditions contained within the documents would unreasonably restrict Buyer's use of the premises or
168   would result in financial obligations unacceptable to Buyer in connection with owning the Real Estate,
169   then Buyer may declare this Contract null and void by giving Seller Notice within five (5) Business Days
170   after the receipt of the documents and information required by Paragraph 14(c), listing those deficiencies
171   which are unacceptable to Buyer. If Notice is not served within the time specified, Buyer shall be deemed
172   to have waived this contingency, and this Contract shall remain in full force and effect.

Buyer Initial _____ Buyer Initial _____ Seller Initial _____ Seller Initial _____

Address _____ v5.0e

173 (e) Seller shall not be obligated to provide a condominium survey.

174 (f) Seller shall provide a certificate of insurance showing Buyer and Buyer's mortgagee, if any, as an insured.

175 **15. THE DEED:** Seller shall convey or cause to be conveyed to Buyer or Buyer's designated grantee good and
176 merchantable title to the Real Estate by recordable general Warranty Deed, with release of homestead rights,
177 (or the appropriate deed if title is in trust or in an estate), and with real estate transfer stamps to be paid by
178 Seller (unless otherwise designated by local ordinance). Title when conveyed will be good and merchantable,
179 subject only to: general real estate taxes not due and payable at the time of Closing; covenants, conditions
180 and restrictions of record; and building lines and easements, if any, provided they do not interfere with the
181 current use and enjoyment of the Real Estate.

182 **16. TITLE:** At Seller's expense, Seller will deliver or cause to be delivered to Buyer or Buyer's attorney within
183 customary time limitations and sufficiently in advance of Closing, as evidence of title in Seller or Grantor, a
184 title commitment for an ALTA title insurance policy in the amount of the Purchase Price with extended
185 coverage by a title company licensed to operate in the State of Illinois, issued on or subsequent to the Date of
186 Acceptance, subject only to items listed in Paragraph 15. The requirement to provide extended coverage shall
187 not apply if the Real Estate is vacant land. The commitment for title insurance furnished by Seller will be
188 conclusive evidence of good and merchantable title as therein shown, subject only to the exceptions therein
189 stated. **If the title commitment discloses any unpermitted exceptions or if the Plat of Survey shows any**
190 **encroachments or other survey matters that are not acceptable to Buyer, then Seller shall have said**
191 **exceptions, survey matters or encroachments removed, or have the title insurer commit to either insure**
192 **against loss or damage that may result from such exceptions or survey matters or insure against any court-**
193 **ordered removal of the encroachments.** If Seller fails to have such exceptions waived or insured over prior to
194 Closing, Buyer may elect to take the title as it then is with the right to deduct from the Purchase Price prior
195 encumbrances of a definite or ascertainable amount. Seller shall furnish Buyer at Closing an Affidavit of Title
196 covering the date of Closing, and shall sign any other customary forms required for issuance of an ALTA
197 Insurance Policy.

198 **17. PLAT OF SURVEY:** Not less than one (1) Business Day prior to Closing, except where the Real Estate is a
199 condominium (see Paragraph 14) Seller shall, at Seller's expense, furnish to Buyer or Buyer's attorney a Plat
200 of Survey that conforms to the current Minimum Standards of Practice for boundary surveys, is dated not
201 more than six (6) months prior to the date of Closing, and is prepared by a professional land surveyor
202 licensed to practice land surveying under the laws of the State of Illinois. The Plat of Survey shall show
203 visible evidence of improvements, rights of way, easements, use and measurements of all parcel lines. The
204 land surveyor shall set monuments or witness corners at all accessible corners of the land. All such corners
205 shall also be visibly staked or flagged. The Plat of Survey shall include the following statement placed near
206 the professional land surveyor seal and signature: "This professional service conforms to the current Illinois
207 Minimum Standards for a boundary survey." A Mortgage Inspection, as defined, is not a boundary survey
208 and is not acceptable.

209 **18. ESCROW CLOSING:** At the election of either Party, not less than five (5) Business Days prior to Closing,
210 this sale shall be closed through an escrow with the lending institution or the title company in accordance
211 with the provisions of the usual form of Deed and Money Escrow Agreement, as agreed upon between the
212 Parties, with provisions inserted in the Escrow Agreement as may be required to conform with this Contract.
213 The cost of the escrow shall be paid by the Party requesting the escrow. If this transaction is a cash purchase
214 (no mortgage is secured by Buyer), the Parties shall share the title company escrow closing fee equally.

215 **19. DAMAGE TO REAL ESTATE OR CONDEMNATION PRIOR TO CLOSING:** If prior to delivery of the deed the
216 Real Estate shall be destroyed or materially damaged by fire or other casualty, or the Real Estate is taken by

Buyer Initial _____   Buyer Initial _____   Seller Initial _____   Seller Initial _____

Address _____ v5.0e

217 condemnation, then Buyer shall have the option of either terminating this Contract (and receiving a refund of
218 earnest money) or accepting the Real Estate as damaged or destroyed, together with the proceeds of the
219 condemnation award or any insurance payable as a result of the destruction or damage, which gross
220 proceeds Seller agrees to assign to Buyer and deliver to Buyer at Closing. Seller shall not be obligated to
221 repair or replace damaged improvements. The provisions of the Uniform Vendor and Purchaser Risk Act of
222 the State of Illinois shall be applicable to this Contract, except as modified by this paragraph.

223 **20. REAL ESTATE TAX ESCROW:** In the event the Real Estate is improved, but has not been previously taxed
224 for the entire year as currently improved, the sum of three percent (3%) of the Purchase Price shall be
225 deposited in escrow with the title company with the cost of the escrow to be divided equally by Buyer and
226 Seller and paid at Closing. When the exact amount of the taxes to be prorated under this Contract can be
227 ascertained, the taxes shall be prorated by Seller's attorney at the request of either Party and Seller's share of
228 such tax liability after proration shall be paid to Buyer from the escrow funds and the balance, if any, shall be
229 paid to Seller. If Seller's obligation after such proration exceeds the amount of the escrow funds, Seller agrees
230 to pay such excess promptly upon demand.

231 **21. SELLER REPRESENTATIONS:** Seller represents that with respect to the Real Estate Seller has no
232 knowledge of nor has Seller received written notice from any governmental body regarding:
233 (a) zoning, building, fire or health code violations that have not been corrected;
234 (b) any pending rezoning;
235 (c) boundary line disputes;
236 (d) any pending condemnation or Eminent Domain proceeding;
237 (e) easements or claims of easements not shown on the public records;
238 (f) any hazardous waste on the Real Estate;
239 (g) any improvements to the Real Estate for which the required permits were not obtained;
240 (h) any improvements to the Real Estate which are not included in full in the determination of the most
241   recent tax assessment; or
242 (i) any improvements to the Real Estate which are eligible for the home improvement tax exemption.

243 Seller further represents that:
244 1. There *[check one]* ❑ is ❑ is not a pending or unconfirmed special assessment affecting the Real Estate by
245   any association or governmental entity payable by Buyer after date of Closing.
246 2. The Real Estate *[check one]* ❑ is ❑ is not located within a Special Assessment Area or Special Service
247   Area, payments for which will not be the obligation of Seller after the year in which the Closing occurs.
248 **If any of the representations contained herein regarding a Special Assessment Area or Special Service**
249 **Area are unacceptable to Buyer, Buyer shall have the option to declare this Contract null and void. If**
250 **Notice of the option to declare this Contract null and void is not given to Seller within ten (10) Business**
251 **Days after the Date of Acceptance or by the Mortgage Contingency deadline date described in Paragraph**
252 **11 (whichever is later), Buyer shall be deemed to have waived such option and this Contract shall remain**
253 **in full force and effect. Seller's representations contained in this paragraph shall survive the Closing.**

254 **22. CONDITION OF REAL ESTATE AND INSPECTION:** Seller agrees to leave the Real Estate in broom clean
255 condition. All refuse and personal property that is not to be conveyed to Buyer shall be removed from the
256 Real Estate at Seller's expense prior to delivery of Possession. Buyer shall have the right to inspect the Real
257 Estate, fixtures and included Personal Property prior to Possession to verify that the Real Estate,
258 improvements and included Personal Property are in substantially the same condition as of the Date of
259 Acceptance, normal wear and tear excepted.

Buyer Initial _____   *Buyer Initial* _____   *Seller Initial* _____   *Seller Initial* _____

Address _____ v5.0

23. MUNICIPAL ORDINANCE, TRANSFER TAX, AND GOVERNMENTAL COMPLIANCE:
(a) Parties are cautioned that the Real Estate may be situated in a municipality that has adopted a pre-closing inspection requirement, municipal Transfer Tax or other similar ordinances. Transfer taxes required by municipal ordinance shall be paid by the party designated in such ordinance.
(b) Parties agree to comply with the reporting requirements of the applicable sections of the Internal Revenue Code and the Real Estate Settlement Procedures Act of 1974, as amended.

24. BUSINESS DAYS/HOURS: Business Days are defined as Monday through Friday, excluding Federal holidays. Business Hours are defined as 8:00 A.M. to 6:00 P.M. Chicago time.

25. FACSIMILE OR DIGITAL SIGNATURES: Facsimile or digital signatures shall be sufficient for purposes of executing, negotiating, and finalizing this Contract.

26. DIRECTION TO ESCROWEE: In every instance where this Contract shall be deemed null and void or if this Contract may be terminated by either Party, the following shall be deemed incorporated: "and earnest money refunded to Buyer upon written direction of the Parties to Escrowee or upon entry of an order by a court of competent jurisdiction". There shall be no disbursement of earnest money unless Escrowee has been provided written direction from Seller and Buyer. Absent a direction relative to the disbursement of earnest money within a reasonable period of time, Escrowee may deposit funds with the Clerk of the Circuit Court by the filing of an action in the nature of Interpleader. Escrowee shall be reimbursed from the earnest money for all costs, including reasonable attorney fees, related to the filing of the Interpleader action. Seller and Buyer shall indemnify and hold Escrowee harmless from any and all conflicting claims and demands arising under this paragraph.

27. NOTICE: Except as provided in Paragraph 31(C)(2) regarding the manner of service for "kick-out" Notices, all Notices shall be in writing and shall be served by one Party or attorney to the other Party or attorney. Notice to any one of a multiple person Party shall be sufficient Notice to all. Notice shall be given in the following manner:
(a) By personal delivery; or
(b) By mailing to the addresses recited herein by regular mail and by certified mail, return receipt requested. Except as otherwise provided herein, Notice served by certified mail shall be effective on the date of mailing; or
(c) By facsimile transmission. Notice shall be effective as of date and time of the transmission, provided that the Notice transmitted shall be sent on Business Days during Business Hours. In the event Notice is transmitted during non-business hours, the effective date and time of Notice is the first hour of the next Business Day after transmission; or
(d) By e-mail transmission if an e-mail address has been furnished by the recipient Party or the recipient Party's attorney to the sending Party or is shown on this Contract. Notice shall be effective as of date and time of e-mail transmission, provided that, in the event e-mail Notice is transmitted during non-business hours, the effective date and time of Notice is the first hour of the next Business Day after transmission. An attorney or Party may opt out of future e-mail Notice by any form of Notice provided by this Contract; or
(e) By commercial overnight delivery (e.g., FedEx). Such Notice shall be effective on the next Business Day following deposit with the overnight delivery company.

28. PERFORMANCE: Time is of the essence of this Contract. In any action with respect to this Contract, the Parties are free to pursue any legal remedies at law or in equity and the prevailing Party in litigation shall be entitled to collect reasonable attorney fees and costs from the non-Prevailing Party as ordered by a court of competent jurisdiction.

| Buyer Initial _____ | Buyer Initial _____ | Seller Initial _____ | Seller Initial _____ |

Address _____ v5.0

304 **29. CHOICE OF LAW/GOOD FAITH:** All terms and provisions of this Contract including but not limited to the
305 Attorney Review and Professional Inspection Paragraphs shall be governed by the laws of the State of Illinois
306 and are subject to the covenant of good faith and fair dealing implied in all Illinois contracts.

307 **30. OTHER PROVISIONS:** This Contract is also subject to those OPTIONAL PROVISIONS initialed by the
308 Parties and the following attachments, if any: _____
309 _____.

310 **OPTIONAL PROVISIONS (Applicable ONLY if initialed by all Parties)**

311 ___ ___ ___ ___ **31. SALE OF BUYER'S REAL ESTATE:**
312 [Initials]
313 **(A) REPRESENTATIONS ABOUT BUYER'S REAL ESTATE:** Buyer represents to Seller as follows:
314   (1) Buyer owns real estate commonly known as (address):
315   _____.
316   (2) Buyer *[check one]* ❏ has ❏ has not entered into a contract to sell said real estate.
317   If Buyer has entered into a contract to sell said real estate, that contract:
318   (a) *[check one]* ❏ is ❏ is not subject to a mortgage contingency.
319   (b) *[check one]* ❏ is ❏ is not subject to a real estate sale contingency.
320   (c) *[check one]* ❏ is ❏ is not subject to a real estate closing contingency.
321   (3) Buyer *[check one]* ❏ has ❏ has not listed said real estate for sale with a licensed real estate broker and
322   in a local multiple listing service.
323   (4) If Buyer's real estate is not listed for sale with a licensed real estate broker and in a local multiple
324   listing service, Buyer *[check one]*
325   (a) ❏ Shall list said real estate for sale with a licensed real estate broker who will place it in a local
326   multiple listing service within five (5) Business Days after the Date of Acceptance.
327   [For information only] Broker: _____
328   Broker's Address: _____ Phone: _____.
329   (b) ❏ Does not intend to list said real estate for sale.
330 **(B) CONTINGENCIES BASED UPON SALE AND/OR CLOSE OF BUYER'S REAL ESTATE:**
331   (1) This Contract is contingent upon Buyer having entered into a contract for the sale of Buyer's real
332   estate that is in full force and effect as of _____, 20___. Such contract should provide
333   for a closing date not later than the Closing Date set forth in this Contract. **If Notice is served on or**
334   **before the date set forth in this subparagraph that Buyer has not procured a contract for the sale of**
335   **Buyer's real estate, this Contract shall be null and void. If Notice that Buyer has not procured a**
336   **contract for the sale of Buyer's real estate is not served on or before the close of business on the**
337   **date set forth in this subparagraph, Buyer shall be deemed to have waived all contingencies**
338   **contained in this Paragraph 31, and this Contract shall remain in full force and effect.** (If this
339   paragraph is used, then the following paragraph **must** be completed.)
340   (2) In the event Buyer has entered into a contract for the sale of Buyer's real estate as set forth in
341   Paragraph 31(B)(1) and that contract is in full force and effect, or has entered into a contract for the
342   sale of Buyer's real estate prior to the execution of this Contract, this Contract is contingent upon
343   Buyer closing the sale of Buyer's real estate on or before _____, 20___. **If Notice that**
344   **Buyer has not closed the sale of Buyer's real estate is served before the close of business on the**
345   **next Business Day after the date set forth in the preceding sentence, this Contract shall be null and**
346   **void. If Notice is not served as described in the preceding sentence, Buyer shall be deemed to have**
347   **waived all contingencies contained in this Paragraph 31, and this Contract shall remain in full**
348   **force and effect.**

| Buyer Initial _____ | Buyer Initial _____ | Seller Initial _____ | Seller Initial _____ |

Address _____ v5.0

8

349 (3) If the contract for the sale of Buyer's real estate is terminated for any reason after the date set forth in
350 Paragraph 31(B)(1) (or after the date of this Contract if no date is set forth in Paragraph 31(B)(1)),
351 Buyer shall, within three (3) Business Days of such termination, notify Seller of said termination.
352 **Unless Buyer, as part of said Notice, waives all contingencies in Paragraph 31 and complies with**
353 **Paragraph 31(D), this Contract shall be null and void as of the date of Notice. If Notice as required**
354 **by this subparagraph is not served within the time specified, Buyer shall be in default under the**
355 **terms of this Contract.**

356 **(C) SELLER'S RIGHT TO CONTINUE TO OFFER REAL ESTATE FOR SALE**: During the time of this contingency,
357 Seller has the right to continue to show the Real Estate and offer it for sale subject to the following:

358 (1) If Seller accepts another bona fide offer to purchase the Real Estate while the contingencies expressed
359 in Paragraph 31(B) are in effect, Seller shall notify Buyer in writing of same. Buyer shall then have
360 _____ hours after Seller gives such Notice to waive the contingencies set forth in Paragraph
361 31(B), subject to Paragraph 31(D).

362 (2) Seller's Notice to Buyer (commonly referred to as a 'kick-out' Notice) shall be in writing and shall be
363 served on Buyer, not Buyer's attorney or Buyer's real estate agent. Courtesy copies of such "kick-out"
364 Notice should be sent to Buyer's attorney and Buyer's real estate agent, if known. Failure to provide
365 such courtesy copies shall not render Notice invalid. Notice to any one of a multiple-person Buyer
366 shall be sufficient Notice to all Buyers. Notice for the purpose of this subparagraph only shall be
367 served upon Buyer in the following manner:
368 (a) By personal delivery effective at the time and date of personal delivery; or
369 (b) By mailing to the addresses recited herein for Buyer by regular mail and by certified mail. Notice
370 shall be effective at 10:00 A.M. on the morning of the second day following deposit of Notice in
371 the U.S. Mail; or
372 (c) By commercial overnight delivery (e.g., FedEx). Notice shall be effective upon delivery or at 4:00
373 P.M. Chicago time on the next delivery day following deposit with the overnight delivery
374 company, whichever first occurs.
375 (3) If Buyer complies with the provisions of Paragraph 31(D) then this Contract shall remain in full force
376 and effect.
377 (4) If the contingencies set forth in Paragraph 31(B) are NOT waived in writing within said time period
378 by Buyer, this Contract shall be null and void.
379 (5) Except as provided in Paragraph 31(C)(2) above, all Notices shall be made in the manner provided by
380 Paragraph 27 of this Contract.
381 (6) Buyer waives any ethical objection to the delivery of Notice under this paragraph by Seller's attorney
382 or representative.

383 **(D) WAIVER OF PARAGRAPH 31 CONTINGENCIES**: Buyer shall be deemed to have waived the contingencies in
384 Paragraph 31(B) when Buyer has delivered written waiver and deposited with the Escrowee additional
385 earnest money in the amount of $_____ in the form of a cashier's or certified check within the
386 time specified. **If Buyer fails to deposit the additional earnest money within the time specified, the waiver**
387 **shall be deemed ineffective and this Contract shall be null and void.**

388 **(E) BUYER COOPERATION REQUIRED:** Buyer authorizes Seller or Seller's agent to verify representations
389 contained in Paragraph 31 at any time, and Buyer agrees to cooperate in providing relevant information.

390 ____ ____ ____ ____ **32. CANCELLATION OF PRIOR REAL ESTATE CONTRACT:** In the event either Party has
391 entered into a prior real estate contract, this Contract shall be subject to written cancellation of the prior
392 contract on or before _____, 20____. **In the event the prior contract is not cancelled within the**
393 **time specified, this Contract shall be null and void. Seller's notice to the purchaser under the prior**

394 contract should not be served until after Attorney Review and Professional Inspections provisions of this
395 Contract have expired, been satisfied or waived.

396 ___ ___ ___ ___ **33. CREDIT AT CLOSING:** Provided Buyer's lender permits such credit to show on the
397 HUD-1 Settlement Statement, **and if not, such lesser amount as the lender permits,** Seller agrees to credit to
398 Buyer at Closing $_____ to be applied to prepaid expenses, closing costs or both.

399 ___ ___ ___ ___ **34. INTEREST BEARING ACCOUNT:** Earnest money (with a completed W-9 and other
400 required forms), shall be held in a federally insured interest bearing account at a financial institution
401 designated by Escrowee. All interest earned on the earnest money shall accrue to the benefit of and be paid to
402 Buyer. **Buyer shall be responsible for any administrative fee (not to exceed $100) charged for setting up the**
403 **account.** In anticipation of Closing, the Parties direct Escrowee to close the account no sooner than ten (10)
404 Business Days prior to the anticipated Closing date.

405 ___ ___ ___ ___ **35. VA OR FHA FINANCING:** If Buyer is seeking VA or FHA financing, this provision shall
406 be applicable: **Required FHA or VA amendments and disclosures shall be attached to this Contract.** If VA,
407 the Funding Fee, or if FHA, the Mortgage Insurance Premium (MIP) shall be paid by Buyer and *[check one]*
408 ❏ shall ❏ shall not be added to the mortgage loan amount.

409 ___ ___ ___ ___ **36. INTERIM FINANCING:** This Contract is contingent upon Buyer obtaining a written
410 commitment for interim financing on or before _____, 20___ in the amount of $_____.
411 **If Buyer is unable to secure the interim financing commitment and gives Notice to Seller within the time**
412 **specified, this Contract shall be null and void. If Notice is not served within the time specified, this**
413 **provision shall be deemed waived by the Parties and this Contract shall remain in full force and effect.**

414 ___ ___ ___ ___ **37. WELL AND/OR SEPTIC/SANITARY INSPECTIONS:** Seller shall obtain at Seller's
415 expense a well water test stating that the well delivers not less than five (5) gallons of water per minute and
416 including a bacteria and nitrate test (and lead test for FHA loans) and/or a septic report from the applicable
417 County Health Department, a Licensed Environmental Health Practitioner, or a licensed well and septic
418 inspector, each dated not more than ninety (90) days prior to Closing, stating that the well and water supply
419 and the private sanitary system are in proper operating condition with no defects noted. Seller shall remedy
420 any defect or deficiency disclosed by said report(s) prior to Closing, provided that if the cost of remedying a
421 defect or deficiency and the cost of landscaping together exceed $3,000.00, and if the Parties cannot reach
422 agreement regarding payment of such additional cost, this Contract may be terminated by either Party.
423 Additional testing recommended by the report shall be obtained at Seller's expense. If the report
424 recommends additional testing after Closing, the Parties shall have the option of establishing an escrow with
425 a mutual cost allocation for necessary repairs or replacements, or either Party may terminate this Contract
426 prior to Closing. Seller shall deliver a copy of such evaluation(s) to Buyer not less than one (1) Business Day
427 prior to Closing.

428 ___ ___ ___ ___ **38. WOOD DESTROYING INFESTATION:** Notwithstanding the provisions of Paragraph 10,
429 within ten (10) Business Days after the Date of Acceptance, Seller at Seller's expense shall deliver to Buyer a
430 written report, dated not more than six (6) months prior to the date of Closing, by a licensed inspector
431 certified by the appropriate state regulatory authority in the subcategory of termites, stating that there is no
432 visible evidence of active infestation by termites or other wood destroying insects. Unless otherwise agreed
433 between the Parties, if the report discloses evidence of active infestation or structural damage, Buyer has the
434 option within five (5) Business Days of receipt of the report to proceed with the purchase or declare this
435 Contract null and void.

Buyer Initial _____	*Buyer Initial* _____	*Seller Initial* _____	*Seller Initial* _____
Address _____			v5.0

436 ___ ___ ___ ___ **39. POST-CLOSING POSSESSION:** Possession shall be delivered no later than 11:59 P.M.
437 on the date that is _____ days after the date of Closing ("the Possession Date"). Seller shall be responsible
438 for all utilities, contents and liability insurance, and home maintenance expenses until delivery of possession.
439 Seller shall deposit in escrow at Closing with _____, *[check one]* ❏ one percent (1%) of the
440 Purchase Price or ❏ the sum of $_____ to be paid by Escrowee as follows:
441 (a) The sum of $_____ per day for use and occupancy from and including the day after
442   Closing to and including the day of delivery of Possession, if on or before the Possession Date;
443 (b) The amount per day equal to three (3) times the daily amount set forth herein shall be paid for each day
444   after the Possession Date specified in this paragraph that Seller remains in possession of the Real Estate;
445   and
446 (c) The balance, if any, to Seller after delivery of Possession and provided that the terms of Paragraph 22
447   have been satisfied. Seller's liability under this paragraph shall not be limited to the amount of the
448   possession escrow deposit referred to above. Nothing herein shall be deemed to create a
449   Landlord / Tenant relationship between the Parties.

450 ___ ___ ___ ___ **40. "AS IS" CONDITION:** This Contract is for the sale and purchase of the Real Estate in its
451 "As Is" condition as of the Date of Offer. Buyer acknowledges that no representations, warranties or
452 guarantees with respect to the condition of the Real Estate have been made by Seller or Seller's Designated
453 Agent other than those known defects, if any, disclosed by Seller. Buyer may conduct an inspection at
454 Buyer's expense. In that event, Seller shall make the Real Estate available to Buyer's inspector at reasonable
455 times. Buyer shall indemnify Seller and hold Seller harmless from and against any loss or damage caused by
456 the acts or negligence of Buyer or any person performing any inspection. **In the event the inspection reveals**
457 **that the condition of the Real Estate is unacceptable to Buyer and Buyer so notifies Seller within five (5)**
458 **Business Days after the Date of Acceptance, this Contract shall be null and void. Failure of Buyer to notify**
459 **Seller or to conduct said inspection operates as a waiver of Buyer's right to terminate this Contract under**
460 **this paragraph and this Contract shall remain in full force and effect.** Buyer acknowledges that the
461 provisions of Paragraph 10 and the warranty provisions of Paragraph 3 do not apply to this Contract.

462 ___ ___ ___ ___ **41. CONFIRMATION OF DUAL AGENCY:** The Parties confirm that they have previously
463 consented to _____
464 (Licensee) acting as a Dual Agent in providing brokerage services on their behalf and specifically consent to
465 Licensee acting as a Dual Agent with regard to the transaction referred to in this Contract.

466 ___ ___ ___ ___ **42. SPECIFIED PARTY APPROVAL:** This Contract is contingent upon the approval of the
467 Real Estate by _____
468 Buyer's Specified Party, within five (5) Business Days after the Date of Acceptance. In the event Buyer's
469 Specified Party does not approve of the Real Estate and Notice is given to Seller within the time specified,
470 this Contract shall be null and void. If Notice is not served within the time specified, this provision shall be
471 deemed waived by the Parties and this Contract shall remain in full force and effect.

472 ___ ___ ___ ___ **43. MISCELLANEOUS PROVISIONS:** Buyer's and Seller's obligations are contingent upon
473 the Parties entering into a separate written agreement consistent with the terms and conditions set forth
474 herein, and with such additional terms as either Party may deem necessary, providing for one or more of the
475 following: *(check applicable boxes)*
476 ❏ Articles of Agreement for Deed or   ❏ Assumption of Seller's Mortgage   ❏ Commercial / Investment
477   Purchase Money Mortgage   ❏ Cooperative Apartment   ❏ New Construction
478 ❏ Short Sale   ❏ Tax-Deferred Exchange   ❏ Vacant Land

Buyer Initial _____	Buyer Initial _____	Seller Initial _____	Seller Initial _____
Address _____			v5.0

479 **THIS DOCUMENT WILL BECOME A LEGALLY BINDING CONTRACT WHEN SIGNED BY ALL PARTIES AND**
480 **DELIVERED TO THE PARTIES OR THEIR AGENTS.**

481 The Parties represent that the text of this form has not been altered and is identical to the official Multi-Board
482 Residential Real Estate Contract 5.0.

483 _____
484 Date of Offer   DATE OF ACCEPTANCE

485 _____
486 Buyer Signature   Seller Signature

487 _____
488 Buyer Signature   Seller Signature

489 _____
490 Print Buyer(s) Name(s) *[Required]*   Print Seller(s) Name(s) *[Required]*

491 _____
492 Address   Address

493 _____
494 City   State   Zip   City   State   Zip

495 _____
496 Phone   E-mail   Phone   E-mail

497   *FOR INFORMATION ONLY*

498 _____
499 Buyer's Broker   MLS #   Seller's Broker   MLS #

500 _____
501 Buyer's Designated Agent   MLS #   Seller's Designated Agent   MLS #

502 _____
503 Phone   Fax   Phone   Fax

504 _____
505 E-mail   E-mail

506 _____
507 Buyer's Attorney   E-mail   Seller's Attorney   E-mail

508 _____
509 Phone   Fax   Phone   Fax

510 _____
511 Mortgage Company   Phone   Homeowner's/Condo Association (if any)   Phone

512 _____
513 Loan Officer   Phone/Fax   Management Co./Other Contact   Phone

514 ©2009, Illinois Real Estate Lawyers Association. All rights reserved. **Unauthorized duplication or alteration of this form or**
515 **any portion thereof is prohibited.** Official form available at www.irela.org (web site of Illinois Real Estate Lawyers
516 Association).

Approved by the following organizations as of July 20, 2009
517 Illinois Real Estate Lawyers Association · DuPage County Bar Association · Will County Bar Association
518 Northwest Suburban Bar Association · Chicago Association of REALTORS®
519 Mainstreet Organization of REALTORS® · Aurora-Tri County Association of REALTORS® · West Towns Board of REALTORS®
520 REALTOR® Association of Northwest Chicagoland · REALTOR® Association of the Fox Valley
521 Oak Park Area Association of REALTORS® · McHenry Association of REALTORS® · Three Rivers Association of REALTORS®
522 North Shore–Barrington Association of REALTORS®

523 **Seller Rejection:** This offer was presented to Seller on _____, 20____ at ____:____ AM/PM
524 and rejected on _____, 20____ at ____:____ AM/PM ____ ____ (Seller initials).

Buyer Initial _____   Buyer Initial _____   Seller Initial _____   Seller Initial _____

Address , _____   v5.0

12

Loan Status Disclosure
Recommended Form - To Be Completed By Loan Officer

Borrowers/Buyers Name(s): _____

Current Address: _____
  Street Address

City or Town _____
  State   Zip

Purchase Price dollar amount prequalified, pre-approved, or approved for:

$_____. Loan Amount $_____ with a total monthly payment not to exceed $_____.

The current status of prequalification or application status of the borrowers/buyers is:

❑ **Prequalification, WITHOUT credit review*:**

The borrowers/buyers listed on this form have **INQUIRED** with our firm about financing to purchase a home and the documentation they provided regarding income and down payment has been reviewed by the loan originator listed below. It is the opinion of said loan originator that the borrowers/buyers should/would qualify for the terms listed in the attached letter.

❑ **Prequalification, WITH credit review*:**

The borrowers/buyers listed on this form have **INQUIRED** with our firm about financing to purchase a home and the documentation of income, down payment and credit report have been reviewed by the loan originator listed below. After careful review, it is the opinion of said loan originator that the borrowers/buyers should/would qualify for the terms listed in the attached letter.
This Prequalification is ❑ **WITH or** ❑ **WITHOUT** Automated Underwriting approval.

❑ **Pre-Approval*:**

The borrowers/buyers have **APPLIED** with our firm for a mortgage loan to purchase a home and the loan application has been approved by an Automated Underwriting System issued or accepted by FNMA, FHLMC, HUD or Nationally recognized purchaser/pooler of mortgage loans, and a conditional commitment has been issued. See attached commitment.

❑ **Approval*:**

The borrowers/buyers have **APPLIED** with our firm for a mortgage loan to purchase a home and the loan application has been reviewed by the actual lender's underwriter and conditional commitment has been issued. See attached commitment.

*Please note that nothing contained herein constitutes a loan commitment or guarantee of financing and is used for disclosure purposes only. See actual commitment letter for specific conditions/requirements of the lender. All approvals are subject to satisfactory appraisal, title, and no material change to borrower(s) financial status.

Information on mortgage company issuing the prequalification, pre-approval or approval:

Originating Company's Name: _____

Company Address: _____
  Street address   City or Town   State   Zip Code

Company Phone: _____ Fax: _____

Loan Originator's name: _____ Date: _____

Loan Originator's signature: _____

Use Recommended by: Illinois Association of Mortgage Professionals;
Illinois Association of REALTORS® and Illinois Real Estate Lawyers Association

E

State Housing Finance Agencies

For information about home buying finance programs available through county and city programs in your state, go to www.dontrent.com.

Alabama Housing Finance Authority
2000 Interstate Park Drive, Suite 408
Montgomery, AL 36109
(334) 244-9200

Alaska Housing Finance Corporation
PO Box 101020
Anchorage, AK 99510
(907) 338-6100

Arkansas Development Finance Authority
PO Box 8023
Little Rock, AR 72203
(501) 682-5900

California Housing Finance Authority
1121 L Street, 7th Floor
Sacramento, CA 95814
(916) 322-3991

Colorado Housing and Finance
Authority
1981 Blake Street
Denver, Colorado 80202-1272
(303) 297-2432

Connecticut Housing Finance
Authority
999 West Street
Rocky Hill, CT 06067-4005
(860) 721-9501

Delaware State Housing
Authority
18 The Green
Dover, DE 19901
(302) 739-4263

Florida Housing Finance
Authority
City Centre Building
227 North Bronough St.,
Suite 5000
Tallahassee, FL 32301-1329
(850) 488-4197

Georgia Department of
Community Affairs/Georgia
Housing & Finance Authority
60 Executive Parkway South,
Suite 250
Atlanta, GA 30329
(404) 679-4840

Hawaii Housing Finance and
Development Corporation
677 Queen St., Suite 300
Honolulu, HI 96813-5120
(808) 587-0640

Idaho Housing Agency
PO Box 7899
Boise, ID 83707
(208) 331-4882

Illinois Housing Development
Authority
401 North Michigan Avenue,
Suite 900
Chicago, IL 60611
(312) 836-5200

Indiana Housing Finance
Authority
Merchants Plaza, South Tower,
Suite 1350
115 W. Washington Street
Indianapolis, IN 46204-3413
(800) 872-0371

Iowa Finance Authority
100 East Grand Avenue,
Suite 250
Des Moines, IA 50309
(515) 242-4990

Kansas Department of
Commerce & Housing
Division of Housing
700 SW Harrison Street,
Suite 1300
Topeka, KS 66603-3712
(785) 296-5865

Kentucky Housing Corporation
1231 Louisville Road
Frankfort, KY 40601
(502) 564-7630

Louisiana Housing Finance
Agency
200 Lafayette St., Suite 300
Baton Rouge, LA 70801
(504) 342-1310

Maine State Housing Authority
353 Water Street
Augusta, ME 04330-4633
(207) 626-4600

Maryland: Department of
Housing & Community
Development/ Maryland
Community Development
Administration
100 Community Place
Crownsville, MD 21032-2023
(410) 514-7007

Massachusetts Housing Finance
Agency
One Beacon Street
Boston, MA 02108
(617) 854-1000

Michigan State Housing
Development Authority
Plaza One Building, 5th Floor
401 South Washington Square
Lansing, MI 48933
(517) 373-6007

Minnesota Housing Finance
Agency
400 Sibley Street, Suite 300
St. Paul, MN 55101
(612) 296-7608

Mississippi Home Corporation
735 Riverside Drive
Jackson, MS 39202
(601) 718-4642

Missouri Housing Development
Commission
3435 Broadway
Kansas City, MO 64111
(816) 759-6600

Montana Board of Housing
836 Front Street
PO Box 200528
Helena, MT 59620
(406) 444-3040

Nebraska Investment Finance
Authority
1230 "O" Street, Suite 200
Lincoln, NE 68508
(402) 434-3900

Nevada Housing Division
1802 Carson Street, Suite 154
Carson City, NV 89701
(702) 687-4258

New Hampshire Housing
Finance Authority
PO Box 5087
Manchester, NH 03108
(603) 472-8623

New Jersey Housing and
Mortgage Finance Agency
637 South Clinton Avenue
PO Box 18550
Trenton, NJ 08650-2085
(609) 278-7400

New Mexico Mortgage Finance
Authority
PO Box 2047
Albuquerque, NM 87103
(505) 843-6880

New York State Housing
Finance Agency
State of New York Mortgage
Agency
641 Lexington Avenue
New York, NY 10022
212-688-4000

North Carolina Housing
Finance Agency
3508 Bush Street
Raleigh, NC 27609-7509
(919) 877-5700

North Dakota Housing Finance
Agency
PO Box 1535
Bismarck, ND 58502
(701) 328-9800

Ohio Housing Finance Agency
77 South High St., 26th Floor
Columbus, OH 43215
(614) 466-7970

Oklahoma Housing Finance
Agency
100 Northwest 63rd, Suite 200
Oklahoma City, OK 73116
(405) 848-1144

Oregon Housing and
Community Services
Department
1600 State Street
Salem, OR 97310-0302
(503) 986-2000

Pennsylvania Housing Finance
Agency
PO Box 8029
Harrisburg, PA 17105
(717) 780-3800

Puerto Rico Housing Finance
Corporation
Call Box 71361
San Juan, PR 00936-1361
(787) 765-7577

Rhode Island Housing and
Mortgage Finance Corporation
44 Washington Street
Providence, RI 02903-1721
(401) 751-5566

South Carolina Housing
Finance and Development
Authority
919 Bluff Road, Suite 300
Columbia, SC 29201
(803) 734-2000

South Dakota Housing
Development Authority
221 South Central
PO Box 1237
Pierre, SD 57501-1237
(605) 773-3181

Tennessee Housing
Development Agency
404 James Robertson Parkway,
Suite 1114
Nashville, TN 37243-0900
(615) 741-2400

Texas Department of Housing
and Community Affairs
PO Box 13941, Suite 300
Austin, TX 78711
(512) 475-3800

Utah Housing Corporation
2479 S. Lake Park Blvd.
West Valley City, UT 84120
(801) 902-8200

Vermont Housing Finance
Agency
PO Box 408
Burlington, VT 05402
(802) 864-5743

Virgin Islands Housing Finance
Authority
PO Box 8760
210-3A Altoona, 1st Floor
St. Thomas, VI 00803
(340) 774-4481

Virginia House Development
Authority
601 South Belvedere Street
Richmond, VA 23220-6504
(804) 782-1986

Washington State Housing
Finance Commission
1000 Second Avenue,
Suite 2700
Seattle, WA 98104-1046
(206) 464-7139

West Virginia Housing
Development Fund
814 Virginia Street, East
Charleston, WV 25301
(304) 345-6475

Wisconsin Housing and
Economic Development
Authority
201 West Washington Avenue,
Suite 700
Madison, WI 53703
(608) 266-7884

Wyoming Community
Development Authority
123 South Durbin Street
Casper, WY 82602
(307) 265-0603

F

Key Internet Information Resources

National Association of Home Builders
www.nahb.org

National Association of REALTORS®
www.realtors.org

National Association of Exclusive Buyer Agents (NAEBA)
www.naeba.org

Federal Housing Administration
www.hud.gov/buying/index.cfm

Fannie Mae
www.fanniemae.com/homebuyers/index.jhtml?&p=Overview

Freddie Mac
http://www.freddiemac.com

Federal Department of Veterans Affairs
www.homeloans.va.gov/

Mortgage Bankers Association
www.homeloanlearningcenter.com

The National Association of Mortgage Brokers (NAMB)
www.namb.org

Nationwide Mortgage Lending Licensing System & Registry
http://mortgage.nationwidelicensingsystem.org

Housing Publications from the Federal Citizen Information Center
www.pueblo.gsa.gov/results.tpl?id1=17&startat=1&--woSECTIONSdatarq=17&--SECTIONSword=ww

Federal Reserve Board
www.federalreserveconsumerhelp.gov/index.cfm?nav=9493

Federal Trade Commission
www.ftc.gov/bcp/menus/consumer/credit/mortgage.shtm

GLOSSARY

Here is a guide to acronyms, phrases, terms and words frequently used in the mortgage industry.

203(b): FHA's single family program which provides mortgage insurance to lenders to protect against the borrower defaulting; 203(b) is used to finance the purchase of new or existing one to four family housing; 203(b) insured loans are known for requiring a low down payment, flexible qualifying guidelines, limited fees, and a limit on maximum loan amount.

203(k): this FHA mortgage insurance program enables homebuyers to finance both the purchase of a house and the cost of its rehabilitation through a single mortgage loan

A

"A" Loan or "A" Paper: a credit rating where the FICO score is 660 or above. There have been no late mortgage payments within a 12-month period. This is the best credit rating to have when entering into a new loan.

ARM: Adjustable Rate Mortgage; a mortgage loan subject to changes in interest rates; when rates change, ARM monthly payments increase or decrease at intervals determined by the lender; the change in monthly payment amount, however, is usually subject to a cap.

Abstract of Title: documents recording the ownership of property throughout time.

Acceleration: the right of the lender to demand payment on the outstanding balance of a loan.

Acceptance: the written approval of the buyer's offer by the seller.

Additional Principal Payment: money paid to the lender in addition to the established payment amount used directly against the loan principal to shorten the length of the loan.

Adjustable-Rate Mortgage (ARM): a mortgage loan that does not have a fixed interest rate. During the life of the loan the interest rate will change based on the index rate. Also referred to as adjustable mortgage loans (AMLs) or variable-rate mortgages (VRMs).

Adjustment Date: the actual date that the interest rate is changed for an ARM.

Adjustment Index: the published market index used to calculate the interest rate of an ARM at the time of origination or adjustment.

Adjustment Interval: the time between the interest rate change and the monthly payment for an ARM. The interval is usually every one, three or five years depending on the index.

Affidavit: a signed, sworn statement made by the buyer or seller regarding the truth of information provided.

Amenity: a feature of the home or property that serves as a benefit to the buyer but that is not necessary to its use; may be natural (like location, woods, water) or man-made (like a swimming pool or garden).

American Society of Home Inspectors: the American Society of Home Inspectors is a professional association of independent home inspectors. Phone: (800) 743-2744

Amortization: a payment plan that enables you to reduce your debt gradually through monthly payments. The payments may be principal and interest, or interest-only. The monthly amount is based on the schedule for the entire term or length of the loan.

Annual Mortgagor Statement: yearly statement to borrowers detailing the remaining principal and amounts paid for taxes and interest.

Annual Percentage Rate (APR): a measure of the cost of credit, expressed as a yearly rate. It includes interest as well as other charges. Because all lenders, by federal law, follow the same rules to ensure the accuracy of the annual percentage rate, it provides consumers with a good basis for comparing the cost of loans, including mortgage plans. APR is a higher rate than the simple interest of the mortgage.

Application: the first step in the official loan approval process; this form is used to record important information about the potential borrower necessary to the underwriting process.

Application Fee: a fee charged by lenders to process a loan application.

Appraisal: a document from a professional that gives an estimate of a property's fair market value based on the sales of comparable homes in the area and the features of a property; an appraisal is generally required by a lender before loan approval to ensure that the mortgage loan amount is not more than the value of the property.

Appraisal Fee: fee charged by an appraiser to estimate the market value of a property.

Appraised Value: an estimation of the current market value of a property.

Appraiser: a qualified individual who uses his or her experience and knowledge to prepare the appraisal estimate.

Appreciation: an increase in property value.

Arbitration: a legal method of resolving a dispute without going to court.

As-is Condition: the purchase or sale of a property in its existing condition without repairs.

Asking Price: a seller's stated price for a property.

Assessed Value: the value that a public official has placed on any asset (used to determine taxes).

Assessments: the method of placing value on an asset for taxation purposes.

Assessor: a government official who is responsible for determining the value of a property for the purpose of taxation.

Assets: any item with measurable value.

Assumable Mortgage: when a home is sold, the seller may be able to transfer the mortgage to the new buyer. This means the mortgage is assumable. Lenders generally require a credit review of the new borrower and may charge a fee for the assumption. Some mortgages contain a due-on-sale clause, which means that the mortgage may not be transferable to a new buyer. Instead, the lender may make you pay the entire balance that is due when you sell the home. An assumable mortgage can help you attract buyers if you sell your home.

Assumption Clause: a provision in the terms of a loan that allows the buyer to take legal responsibility for the mortgage from the seller.

Automated Underwriting: loan processing completed through a computer-based system that evaluates past credit history to determine if a loan should be approved. This system removes the possibility of personal bias against the buyer.

Average Price: determining the cost of a home by totaling the cost of all houses sold in one area and dividing by the number of homes sold.

B

"B" Loan or "B" Paper: FICO scores from 620 - 659. Factors include two 30 day late mortgage payments and two to three 30 day late installment loan payments in the last 12 months. No delinquencies over 60 days are allowed. Should be two to four years since a bankruptcy. Also referred to as Sub-Prime.

Back End Ratio (debt ratio): a ratio that compares the total of all monthly debt payments (mortgage, real estate taxes and insurance, car loans, and other consumer loans) to gross monthly income.

Back to Back Escrow: arrangements that an owner makes to oversee the sale of one property and the purchase of another at the same time.

Balance Sheet: a financial statement that shows the assets, liabilities and net worth of an individual or company.

Balloon Loan or Mortgage: a mortgage that typically offers low rates for an initial period of time (usually 5, 7, or 10) years; after that time period elapses, the balance is due or is refinanced by the borrower.

Balloon Payment: the final lump sum payment due at the end of a balloon mortgage.

Bankruptcy: a federal law whereby a person's assets are turned over to a trustee and used to pay off outstanding debts; this usually occurs when someone owes more than they have the ability to repay.

Biweekly Payment Mortgage: a mortgage paid twice a month instead of once a month, reducing the amount of interest to be paid on the loan.

Borrower: a person who has been approved to receive a loan and is then obligated to repay it and any additional fees according to the loan terms.

Bridge Loan: a short-term loan paid back relatively fast. Normally used until a long-term loan can be processed.

Broker: a licensed individual or firm that charges a fee to serve as the mediator between the buyer and seller. Mortgage brokers are individuals in the business of arranging funding or negotiating contracts for a client, but who does not loan the money. A real estate broker is someone who helps find a house.

Building Code: based on agreed upon safety standards within a specific area, a building code is a regulation that determines the design, construction, and materials used in building.

Budget: a detailed record of all income earned and spent during a specific period of time.

Buy Down: the seller pays an amount to the lender so the lender provides a lower rate and lower payments many times for an ARM. The seller may increase the sales price to cover the cost of the buy down.

C

"C" Loan or "C" Paper: FICO scores typically from 580 to 619. Factors include three to four 30 day late mortgage payments and four to six 30 day late installment loan payments or two to four 60 day late payments. Should be one to two years since bankruptcy. Also referred to as Sub - Prime.

Callable Debt: a debt security whose issuer has the right to redeem the security at a specified price on or after a specified date, but prior to its stated final maturity.

Cap: a limit, such as one placed on an adjustable rate mortgage, on how much a monthly payment or interest rate can increase or decrease, either at each adjustment period or during the life of the mortgage. Payment caps do not limit the amount of interest the lender is earning, so they may cause negative amortization.

Capacity: The ability to make mortgage payments on time, dependant on assets and the amount of income each month after paying housing costs, debts and other obligations.

Capital Gain: the profit received based on the difference of the original purchase price and the total sale price.

Capital Improvements: property improvements that either will enhance the property value or will increase the useful life of the property.

Capital or Cash Reserves: an individual's savings, investments, or assets.

Cash-Out Refinance: when a borrower refinances a mortgage at a higher principal amount to get additional money. Usually this occurs when the property has appreciated in value. For example, if a home has a current value of $100,000 and an outstanding mortgage of $60,000, the owner could refinance $80,000 and have additional $20,000 in cash.

Cash Reserves: a cash amount sometimes required of the buyer to be held in reserve in addition to the down payment and closing costs; the amount is determined by the lender.

Casualty Protection: property insurance that covers any damage to the home and personal property either inside or outside the home.

Certificate of Title: a document provided by a qualified source, such as a title company, that shows the property legally belongs to the current owner; before the title is transferred at closing, it should be clear and free of all liens or other claims.

Chapter 7 Bankruptcy: a bankruptcy that requires assets be liquidated in exchange for the cancellation of debt.

Chapter 13 Bankruptcy: this type of bankruptcy sets a payment plan between the borrower and the creditor monitored by the court. The homeowner can keep the property, but must make payments according to the court's terms within a 3 to 5 year period.

Charge-Off: the portion of principal and interest due on a loan that is written off when deemed to be uncollectible.

Clear Title: a property title that has no defects. Properties with clear titles are marketable for sale.

Closing: the final step in property purchase where the title is transferred from the seller to the buyer. Closing occurs at a meeting between the buyer, seller, settlement agent, and other agents. At the closing the seller receives payment for the property. Also known as settlement.

Closing Costs: fees for final property transfer not included in the price of the property. Typical closing costs include charges for the mortgage loan such as origination fees, discount points, appraisal fee, survey, title insurance, legal fees, real estate professional fees, prepayment of taxes and insurance, and real estate transfer taxes. A common estimate of a Buyer's closing costs is 2 to 4 percent of the purchase price of the home. A common estimate for Seller's closing costs is 3 to 9 percent.

Cloud On The Title: any condition which affects the clear title to real property.

Co-Borrower: an additional person that is responsible for loan repayment and is listed on the title.

Co-Signed Account: an account signed by someone in addition to the primary borrower, making both people responsible for the amount borrowed.

Co-Signer: a person that signs a credit application with another person, agreeing to be equally responsible for the repayment of the loan.

Collateral: security in the form of money or property pledged for the payment of a loan. For example, on a home loan, the home is the collateral and can be taken away from the borrower if mortgage payments are not made.

Collection Account: an unpaid debt referred to a collection agency to collect on the bad debt. This type of account is reported to the credit bureau and will show on the borrower's credit report.

Commission: an amount, usually a percentage of the property sales price that is collected by a real estate professional as a fee for negotiating the transaction. Traditionally the home seller pays the commission. The amount of commission is determined by the real estate professional and the seller and can be as much as 6% of the sales price.

Common Stock: a security that provides voting rights in a corporation and pays a dividend after preferred stock holders have been paid. This is the most common stock held within a company.

Comparative Market Analysis (COMPS): a property evaluation that determines property value by comparing similar properties sold within the last year.

Compensating Factors: factors that show the ability to repay a loan based on less traditional criteria, such as employment, rent, and utility payment history.

Condominium: a form of ownership in which individuals purchase and own a unit of housing in a multi-unit complex. The owner also shares financial responsibility for common areas.

Conforming loan: is a loan that does not exceed Fannie Mae's and Freddie Mac's loan limits. Freddie Mac and Fannie Mae loans are referred to as conforming loans.

Consideration: an item of value given in exchange for a promise or act.

Construction Loan: a short-term, to finance the cost of building a new home. The lender pays the builder based on milestones accomplished during the building process. For example, once a sub-contractor pours the foundation and it is approved by inspectors the lender will pay for their service.

Contingency: a clause in a purchase contract outlining conditions that must be fulfilled before the contract is executed. Both, buyer or seller may include contingencies in a contract, but both parties must accept the contingency.

Conventional Loan: a private sector loan, one that is not guaranteed or insured by the U.S. government.

Conversion Clause: a provision in some ARMs allowing it to change to a fixed-rate loan at some point during the term. Usually conversions are allowed at the end of the first adjustment period. At the time of the conversion, the new fixed rate is generally set at one of the rates then prevailing for fixed rate mortgages. There may be additional cost for this clause.

Convertible ARM: an adjustable-rate mortgage that provides the borrower the ability to convert to a fixed-rate within a specified time.

Cooperative (Co-op): residents purchase stock in a cooperative corporation that owns a structure; each stockholder is then entitled to live in a specific unit of the structure and is responsible for paying a portion of the loan.

Cost of Funds Index (COFI): an index used to determine interest rate changes for some adjustable-rate mortgages.

Counter Offer: a rejection to all or part of a purchase offer that negotiates different terms to reach an acceptable sales contract.

Covenants: legally enforceable terms that govern the use of property. These terms are transferred with the property deed. Discriminatory covenants are illegal and unenforceable. Also known as a condition, restriction, deed restriction or restrictive covenant.

Credit: an agreement that a person will borrow money and repay it to the lender over time.

Credit Bureau: an agency that provides financial information and payment history to lenders about potential borrowers. Also known as a National Credit Repository.

Credit Counseling: education on how to improve bad credit and how to avoid having more debt than can be repaid.

Credit Enhancement: a method used by a lender to reduce default of a loan by requiring collateral, mortgage insurance, or other agreements.

Credit Grantor: the lender that provides a loan or credit.

Credit History: a record of an individual that lists all debts and the payment history for each. The report that is generated from the history is called a credit report. Lenders use this information to gauge a potential borrower's ability to repay a loan.

Credit Loss Ratio: the ratio of credit-related losses to the dollar amount of MBS outstanding and total mortgages owned by the corporation.

Credit Related Expenses: foreclosed property expenses plus the provision for losses.

Credit Related Losses: foreclosed property expenses combined with charge-offs.

Credit Repair Companies: Private, for-profit businesses that claim to offer consumers credit and debt repayment difficulties assistance with their credit problems and a bad credit report.

Credit Report: a report generated by the credit bureau that contains the borrower's credit history for the past seven years. Lenders use this information to determine if a loan will be granted.

Credit Risk: a term used to describe the possibility of default on a loan by a borrower.

Credit Score: a score calculated by using a person's credit report to determine the likelihood of a loan being repaid on time. Scores range from about 360 - 840: a lower score meaning a person is a higher risk, while a higher score means that there is less risk.

Credit Union: a non-profit financial institution federally regulated and owned by the members or people who use their services. Credit unions serve groups that hold a common interest and you have to become a member to use the available services.

Creditor: the lending institution providing a loan or credit.

Creditworthiness: the way a lender measures the ability of a person to qualify and repay a loan.

D

Debtor: The person or entity that borrows money. The term debtor may be used interchangeably with the term borrower.

Debt-to-Income Ratio: a comparison or ratio of gross income to housing and non-housing expenses; With the FHA, the-monthly mortgage payment should be no more than 29% of monthly gross income (before taxes) and the mortgage payment combined with non-housing debts should not exceed 41% of income.

Debt Security: a security that represents a loan from an investor to an issuer. The issuer in turn agrees to pay interest in addition to the principal amount borrowed.

Deductible: the amount of cash payment that is made by the insured (the homeowner) to cover a portion of a damage or loss. Sometimes also called "out-of-pocket expenses." For example, out of a total damage claim of $1,000, the homeowner might pay a $250 deductible toward the loss, while the insurance company pays $750 toward the loss. Typically, the higher the deductible, the lower the cost of the policy.

Deed: a document that legally transfers ownership of property from one person to another. The deed is recorded on public record with the property description and the owner's signature. Also known as the title.

Deed-in-Lieu: to avoid foreclosure ("in lieu" of foreclosure), a deed is given to the lender to fulfill the obligation to repay the debt; this process does not allow the borrower to remain in the house but helps avoid the costs, time, and effort associated with foreclosure.

Default: the inability to make timely monthly mortgage payments or otherwise comply with mortgage terms. A loan is considered in default when payment has not been paid after 60 to 90 days. Once in default the lender can exercise legal rights defined in the contract to begin foreclosure proceedings

Delinquency: failure of a borrower to make timely mortgage payments under a loan agreement. Generally after fifteen days a late fee may be assessed.

Deposit (Earnest Money): money put down by a potential buyer to show that they are serious about purchasing the home; it becomes part of the down payment if the offer is accepted, is returned if the offer is rejected, or is forfeited if the buyer pulls out of the deal.

During the contingency period the money may be returned to the buyer if the contingencies are not met to the buyer's satisfaction.

Depreciation: a decrease in the value or price of a property due to changes in market conditions, wear and tear on the property, or other factors.

Derivative: a contract between two or more parties where the security is dependent on the price of another investment.

Disclosures: the release of relevant information about a property that may influence the final sale, especially if it represents defects or problems. "Full disclosure" usually refers to the responsibility of the seller to voluntarily provide all known information about the property. Some disclosures may be required by law, such as the federal requirement to warn of potential lead-based paint hazards in pre-1978 housing. A seller found to have knowingly lied about a defect may face legal penalties.

Discount Point: normally paid at closing and generally calculated to be equivalent to 1% of the total loan amount, discount points are paid to reduce the interest rate on a loan. In an ARM with an initial rate discount, the lender gives up a number of percentage points in interest to give you a lower rate and lower payments for part of the mortgage term (usually for one year or less). After the discount period, the ARM rate will probably go up depending on the index rate.

Down Payment: the portion of a home's purchase price that is paid in cash and is not part of the mortgage loan. This amount varies based on the loan type, but is determined by taking the difference of the sale price and the actual mortgage loan amount. Mortgage insurance is required when a down payment less than 20 percent is made.

Document Recording: after closing on a loan, certain documents are filed and made public record. Discharges for the prior mortgage holder are filed first. Then the deed is filed with the new owner's and mortgage company's names.

Due on Sale Clause: a provision of a loan allowing the lender to demand full repayment of the loan if the property is sold.

Duration: the number of years it will take to receive the present value of all future payments on a security to include both principal and interest.

E

Earnest Money (Deposit): money put down by a potential buyer to show that they are serious about purchasing the home; it becomes part of the down payment if the offer is accepted, is returned if the offer is rejected, or is forfeited if the buyer pulls out of the deal. During the contingency period the money may be returned to the buyer if the contingencies are not met to the buyer's satisfaction.

Earnings Per Share (EPS): a corporation's profit that is divided among each share of common stock. It is determined by taking the net earnings divided by the number of outstanding common stocks held. This is a way that a company reports profitability.

Easements: the legal rights that give someone other than the owner access to use property for a specific purpose. Easements may affect property values and are sometimes a part of the deed.

EEM: Energy Efficient Mortgage; an FHA program that helps home-buyers save money on utility bills by enabling them to finance the cost of adding energy efficiency features to a new or existing home as part of the home purchase

Eminent Domain: when a government takes private property for public use. The owner receives payment for its fair market value. The property can then proceed to condemnation proceedings.

Encroachments: a structure that extends over the legal property line on to another individual's property. The property surveyor will note any encroachment on the lot survey done before property transfer. The person who owns the structure will be asked to remove it to prevent future problems.

Encumbrance: anything that affects title to a property, such as loans, leases, easements, or restrictions.

Equal Credit Opportunity Act (ECOA): a federal law requiring lenders to make credit available equally without discrimination based on race, color, religion, national origin, age, sex, marital status, or receipt of income from public assistance programs.

Equity: an owner's financial interest in a property; calculated by subtracting the amount still owed on the mortgage loon(s)from the fair market value of the property.

Escape Clause: a provision in a purchase contract that allows either party to cancel part or the entire contract if the other does not respond to changes to the sale within a set period. The most common use of the escape clause is if the buyer makes the purchase offer contingent on the sale of another house.

Escrow: funds held in an account to be used by the lender to pay for home insurance and property taxes. The funds may also be held by a third party until contractual conditions are met and then paid out.

Escrow Account: a separate account into which the lender puts a portion of each monthly mortgage payment; an escrow account provides the funds needed for such expenses as property taxes, homeowners insurance, mortgage insurance, etc.

Estate: the ownership interest of a person in real property. The sum total of all property, real and personal, owned by a person.

Exclusive Listing: a written contract giving a real estate agent the exclusive right to sell a property for a specific timeframe.

F

FICO Score: FICO is an abbreviation for Fair Isaac Corporation and refers to a person's credit score based on credit history. Lenders and credit card companies use the number to decide if the person is likely to pay his or her bills. A credit score is evaluated using information from the three major credit bureaus and is usually between 300 and 850.

FSBO (For Sale by Owner): a home that is offered for sale by the owner without the benefit of a real estate professional.

Fair Credit Reporting Act: federal act to ensure that credit bureaus are fair and accurate protecting the individual's privacy rights enacted in 1971 and revised in October 1997.

Fair Housing Act: a law that prohibits discrimination in all facets of the home buying process on the basis of race, color, national origin, religion, sex, familial status, or disability.

Fair Market Value: the hypothetical price that a willing buyer and seller will agree upon when they are acting freely, carefully, and with complete knowledge of the situation.

Familial Status: HUD uses this term to describe a single person, a pregnant woman or a household with children under 18 living with parents or legal custodians who might experience housing discrimination.

Fannie Mae: Federal National Mortgage Association (FNMA); a federally-chartered enterprise owned by private stockholders that purchases residential mortgages and converts them into securities for sale to investors; by purchasing mortgages, Fannie Mae supplies funds that lenders may loan to potential homebuyers. Also known as a Government Sponsored Enterprise (GSE).

FHA: Federal Housing Administration; established in 1934 to advance homeownership opportunities for all Americans; assists homebuyers by providing mortgage insurance to lenders to cover most losses that may occur when a borrower defaults; this encourages lenders to make loans to borrowers who might not qualify for conventional mortgages.

First Mortgage: the mortgage with first priority if the loan is not paid.

Fixed Expenses: payments that do not vary from month to month.

Fixed-Rate Mortgage: a mortgage with payments that remain the same throughout the life of the loan because the interest rate and other terms are fixed and do not change.

Fixture: personal property permanently attached to real estate or real property that becomes a part of the real estate.

Float: the act of allowing an interest rate and discount points to fluctuate with changes in the market.

Flood Insurance: insurance that protects homeowners against losses from a flood; if a home is located in a flood plain, the lender will require flood insurance before approving a loan.

Forbearance: a lender may decide not to take legal action when a borrower is late in making a payment. Usually this occurs when a borrower sets up a plan that both sides agree will bring overdue mortgage payments up to date.

Foreclosure: a legal process in which mortgaged property is sold to pay the loan of the defaulting borrower. Foreclosure laws are based on the statutes of each state.

Freddie Mac: Federal Home Loan Mortgage Corporation (FHLM); a federally chartered corporation that purchases residential mortgages, securitizes them, and sells them to investors; this provides lenders with funds for new homebuyers. Also known as a Government Sponsored Enterprise (GSE).

Front End Ratio: a percentage comparing a borrower's total monthly cost to buy a house (mortgage principal and interest, insurance, and real estate taxes) to monthly income before deductions.

G

GSE: abbreviation for government sponsored enterprises: a collection of financial services corporations formed by the United States Congress to reduce interest rates for farmers and homeowners. Examples include Fannie Mae and Freddie Mac.

Ginnie Mae: Government National Mortgage Association (GNMA); a government-owned corporation overseen by the U.S. Department of Housing and Urban Development, Ginnie Mae pools FHA-insured and VA-guaranteed loans to back securities for private investment; as With Fannie Mae and Freddie Mac, the investment income provides funding that may then be lent to eligible borrowers by lenders.

Global Debt Facility: designed to allow investors all over the world to purchase debt (loans) of U.S. dollar and foreign currency through a variety of clearing systems.

Good Faith Estimate: an estimate of all closing fees including prepaid and escrow items as well as lender charges; must be given to the borrower within three days after submission of a loan application.

Graduated Payment Mortgages: mortgages that begin with lower monthly payments that get slowly larger over a period of years, eventually reaching a fixed level and remaining there for the life of the loan. Graduated payment loans may be good if you expect your annual income to increase.

Grantee: an individual to whom an interest in real property is conveyed.

Grantor: an individual conveying an interest in real property.

Gross Income: money earned before taxes and other deductions. Sometimes it may include income from self-employment, rental property, alimony, child support, public assistance payments, and retirement benefits.

Guaranty Fee: payment to FannieMae from a lender for the assurance of timely principal and interest payments to MBS (Mortgage Backed Security) security holders.

H

HECM (Reverse Mortgage): the reverse mortgage is used by senior homeowners age 62 and older to convert the equity in their home into monthly streams of income and/or a line of credit to be repaid when they no longer occupy the home. A lending institution such as a mortgage lender, bank, credit union or savings and loan association funds the FHA insured loan, commonly known as HECM.

Hazard Insurance: protection against a specific loss, such as fire, wind etc., over a period of time that is secured by the payment of a regularly scheduled premium.

HELP: Homebuyer Education Learning Program; an educational program from the FHA that counsels people about the home buying process; HELP covers topics like budgeting, finding a home, getting a loan, and home maintenance; in most cases, completion of the program may entitle the homebuyer to a reduced initial FHA mortgage insurance premium-from 2.25% to 1.75% of the home purchase price.

Home Equity Line of Credit: a mortgage loan, usually in second mortgage, allowing a borrower to obtain cash against the equity of a home, up to a predetermined amount.

Home Equity Loan: a loan backed by the value of a home (real estate). If the borrower defaults or does not pay the loan, the lender has some rights to the property. The borrower can usually claim a home equity loan as a tax deduction.

Home Inspection: an examination of the structure and mechanical systems to determine a home's quality, soundness and safety; makes the potential homebuyer aware of any repairs that may be needed. The homebuyer generally pays inspection fees.

Home Warranty: offers protection for mechanical systems and attached appliances against unexpected repairs not covered by homeowner's insurance; coverage extends over a specific time period and does not cover the home's structure.

Homeowner's Insurance: an insurance policy, also called hazard insurance, that combines protection against damage to a dwelling and its contents including fire, storms or other damages with protection against claims of negligence or inappropriate action that result in someone's injury or property damage. Most lenders require homeowners insurance and may escrow the cost. Flood insurance is generally not included in standard policies and must be purchased separately.

Homeownership Education Classes: classes that stress the need to develop a strong credit history and offer information about how to get a mortgage approved, qualify for a loan, choose an affordable home, go through financing and closing processes, and avoid mortgage problems that cause people to lose their homes.

Homestead Credit: property tax credit program, offered by some state governments, that provides reductions in property taxes to eligible households.

Housing Counseling Agency: provides counseling and assistance to individuals on a variety of issues, including loan default, fair housing, and home buying.

HUD: the U.S. Department of Housing and Urban Development; established in 1965, HUD works to create a decent home and suitable living environment for all Americans; it does this by addressing housing needs, improving and developing American communities, and enforcing fair housing laws.

HUD1 Statement: also known as the "settlement sheet," or "closing statement" it itemizes all closing costs; must be given to the borrower at or before closing. Items that appear on the statement include real estate commissions, loan fees, points, and escrow amounts.

HVAC: Heating, Ventilation and Air Conditioning; a home's heating and cooling system.

I

Indemnification: to secure against any loss or damage, compensate or give security for reimbursement for loss or damage incurred. A homeowner should negotiate for inclusion of an indemnification provision in a contract with a general contractor or for a separate indemnity agreement protecting the homeowner from harm, loss or damage caused by actions or omissions of the general (and all sub) contractor.

Index: the measure of interest rate changes that the lender uses to decide how much the interest rate of an ARM will change over time. No one can be sure when an index rate will go up or down. If a lender bases interest rate adjustments on the average value of an index over time, your interest rate would not be as volatile. You should ask your lender how the index for any ARM you are considering has changed in recent years, and where it is reported.

Inflation: the number of dollars in circulation exceeds the amount of goods and services available for purchase; inflation results in a decrease in the dollar's value.

Inflation Coverage: endorsement to a homeowner's policy that automatically adjusts the amount of insurance to compensate for inflationary rises in the home's value. This type of coverage does not adjust for increases in the home's value due to improvements.

Inquiry: a credit report request. Each time a credit application is completed or more credit is requested counts as an inquiry. A large number of inquiries on a credit report can sometimes make a credit score lower.

Interest: a fee charged for the use of borrowing money.

Interest Rate: the amount of interest charged on a monthly loan payment, expressed as a percentage.

Interest Rate Swap: a transaction between two parties where each agrees to exchange payments tied to different interest rates for a specified period of time, generally based on a notional principal amount.

Intermediate Term Mortgage: a mortgage loan with a contractual maturity from the time of purchase equal to or less than 20 years.

Insurance: protection against a specific loss, such as fire, wind etc., over a period of time that is secured by the payment of a regularly scheduled premium.

J

Joint Tenancy (with Rights of Survivorship): two or more owners share equal ownership and rights to the property. If a joint owner dies, his or her share of the property passes to the other owners, without probate. In joint tenancy, ownership of the property cannot be willed to someone who is not a joint owner.

Judgment: a legal decision; when requiring debt repayment, a judgment may include a property lien that secures the creditor's claim by providing a collateral source.

Jumbo Loan: or non-conforming loan, is a loan that exceeds Fannie Mae's and Freddie Mac's loan limits. Freddie Mac and Fannie Mae loans are referred to as conforming loans.

L

Late Payment Charges: the penalty the homeowner must pay when a mortgage payment is made after the due date grace period.

Lease: a written agreement between a property owner and a tenant (resident) that stipulates the payment and conditions under which the tenant may occupy a home or apartment and states a specified period of time.

Lease Purchase (Lease Option): assists low to moderate income homebuyers in purchasing a home by allowing them to lease a home with an option to buy; the rent payment is made up of the monthly rental payment plus an additional amount that is credited to an account for use as a down payment.

Lender: A term referring to an person or company that makes loans for real estate purchases. Sometimes referred to as a loan officer or lender.

Lender Option Commitments: an agreement giving a lender the option to deliver loans or securities by a certain date at agreed upon terms.

Liabilities: a person's financial obligations such as long-term / short-term debt, and other financial obligations to be paid.

Liability Insurance: insurance coverage that protects against claims alleging a property owner's negligence or action resulted in bodily injury or damage to another person. It is normally included in home-owner's insurance policies.

Lien: a legal claim against property that must be satisfied when the property is sold. A claim of money against a property, wherein the value of the property is used as security in repayment of a debt. Examples include a mechanic's lien, which might be for the unpaid cost of building supplies, or a tax lien for unpaid property taxes. A lien is a defect on the title and needs to be settled before transfer of ownership. A lien release is a written report of the settlement of a lien and is recorded in the public record as evidence of payment.

Lien Waiver: A document that releases a consumer (homeowner) from any further obligation for payment of a debt once it has been paid in full. Lien waivers typically are used by homeowners who hire a contractor to provide work and materials to prevent any subcontractors or suppliers of materials from filing a lien against the homeowner for nonpayment.

Life Cap: a limit on the range interest rates can increase or decrease over the life of an adjustable-rate mortgage (ARM).

Line of Credit: an agreement by a financial institution such as a bank to extend credit up to a certain amount for a certain time to a specified borrower.

Liquid Asset: a cash asset or an asset that is easily converted into cash.

Listing Agreement: a contract between a seller and a real estate professional to market and sell a home. A listing agreement obligates the real estate professional (or his or her agent) to seek qualified buyers, report all purchase offers and help negotiate the highest possible price and most favorable terms for the property seller.

Loan: money borrowed that is usually repaid with interest.

Loan Acceleration: an acceleration clause in a loan document is a statement in a mortgage that gives the lender the right to demand payment of the entire outstanding balance if a monthly payment is missed.

Loan Fraud: purposely giving incorrect information on a loan application in order to better qualify for a loan; may result in civil liability or criminal penalties.

Loan Officer: a representative of a lending or mortgage company who is responsible for soliciting homebuyers, qualifying and processing of loans. They may also be called lender, loan representative, account executive or loan rep.

Loan Origination Fee: a charge by the lender to cover the administrative costs of making the mortgage. This charge is paid at the closing and varies with the lender and type of loan. A loan origination fee of 1 to 2 percent of the mortgage amount is common.

Loan Servicer: the company that collects monthly mortgage payments and disperses property taxes and insurance payments. Loan servicers also monitor nonperforming loans, contact delinquent borrowers, and notify insurers and investors of potential problems. Loan servicers may be the lender or a specialized company that just handles loan servicing under contract with the lender or the investor who owns the loan.

Loan to Value (LTV) Ratio: a percentage calculated by dividing the amount borrowed by the price or appraised value of the home to be purchased; the higher the LTV, the less cash a borrower is required to pay as down payment.

Lock-In: since interest rates can change frequently, many lenders offer an interest rate lock-in that guarantees a specific interest rate if the loan is closed within a specific time.

Lock-in Period: the length of time that the lender has guaranteed a specific interest rate to a borrower.

Loss Mitigation: a process to avoid foreclosure; the lender tries to help a borrower who has been unable to make loan payments and is in danger of defaulting on his or her loan

M

Mandatory Delivery Commitment: an agreement that a lender will deliver loans or securities by a certain date at agreed-upon terms.

Margin: the number of percentage points the lender adds to the index rate to calculate the ARM interest rate at each adjustment.

Market Value: the amount a willing buyer would pay a willing seller for a home. An appraised value is an estimate of the current fair market value.

Maturity: the date when the principal balance of a loan becomes due and payable.

Median Price: the price of the house that falls in the middle of the total number of homes for sale in that area.

Medium Term Notes: unsecured general obligations of Fannie Mae with maturities of one day or more and with principal and interest payable in U.S. dollars.

Merged Credit Report: raw data pulled from two or more of the major credit-reporting firms.

Mitigation: term usually used to refer to various changes or improvements made in a home; for instance, to reduce the average level of radon.

Modification: when a lender agrees to modify the terms of a mortgage without refinancing the loan.

Mortgage: a lien on the property that secures the Promise to repay a loan. A security agreement between the lender and the buyer in which the property is collateral for the loan. The mortgage gives the lender the right to collect payment on the loan and to foreclose if the loan obligations are not met.

Mortgage Acceleration Clause: a clause allowing a lender, under certain circumstances, demand the entire balance of a loan is repaid in a lump sum. The acceleration clause is usually triggered if the home is sold, title to the property is changed, the loan is refinanced or the borrower defaults on a scheduled payment.

Mortgage-Backed Security (MBS): a Fannie Mae security that represents an undivided interest in a group of mortgages. Principal and interest payments from the individual mortgage loans are grouped and paid out to the MBS holders.

Mortgage Banker: a company that originates loans and resells them to secondary mortgage lenders like Fannie Mae or Freddie Mac.

Mortgage Broker: a firm that originates and processes loans for a number of lenders.

Mortgage Life and Disability Insurance: term life insurance bought by borrowers to pay off a mortgage in the event of death or make monthly payments in the case of disability. The amount of coverage decreases as the principal balance declines. There are many different terms of coverage determining amounts of payments and when payments begin and end.

Mortgage Insurance: a policy that protects lenders against some or most of the losses that can occur when a borrower defaults on a mortgage loan; mortgage insurance is required primarily for borrowers with a down payment of less than 20% of the home's purchase price. Insurance purchased by the buyer to protect the lender in the event of default. Typically purchased for loans with less than 20 percent down payment. The cost of mortgage insurance is usually added to the monthly payment. Mortgage insurance is maintained on conventional loans until the outstanding amount of the loan is less than 80 percent of the value of the house or for a set period of time (7 years is common). Mortgage insurance also is available through a government agency, such as the Federal Housing Administration (FHA) or through companies (Private Mortgage Insurance or PMI).

Mortgage Insurance Premium (MIP): a monthly payment -usually part of the mortgage payment - paid by a borrower for mortgage insurance.

Mortgage Interest Deduction: the interest cost of a mortgage, which is a tax - deductible expense. The interest reduces the taxable income of taxpayers.

Mortgage Modification: a loss mitigation option that allows a borrower to refinance and/or extend the term of the mortgage loan and thus reduce the monthly payments.

Mortgage Note: a legal document obligating a borrower to repay a loan at a stated interest rate during a specified period; the agreement is secured by a mortgage that is recorded in the public records along with the deed.

Mortgage Qualifying Ratio: Used to calculate the maximum amount of funds that an individual traditionally may be able to afford. A typical mortgage qualifying ratio is 28: 36.

Mortgage Score: a score based on a combination of information about the borrower that is obtained from the loan application, the credit report, and property value information. The score is a comprehensive analysis of the borrower's ability to repay a mortgage loan and manage credit.

Mortgagee: the lender in a mortgage agreement. Mortgagor - The borrower in a mortgage agreement.

Mortgagor: the borrower in a mortgage agreement

Multifamily Housing: a building with more than four residential rental units.

Multiple Listing Service (MLS): within the Metro Columbus area, Realtors submit listings and agree to attempt to sell all properties in the MLS. The MLS is a service of the local Columbus Board of Realtors?. The local MLS has a protocol for updating listings and sharing commissions. The MLS offers the advantage of more timely information, availability, and access to houses and other types of property on the market.

N

National Credit Repositories: currently, there are three companies that maintain national credit - reporting databases. These are Equifax, Experian, and Trans Union, referred to as Credit Bureaus.

Negative Amortization: amortization means that monthly payments are large enough to pay the interest and reduce the principal on your mortgage. Negative amortization occurs when the monthly payments do not cover all of the interest cost. The interest cost that isn't covered is added to the unpaid principal balance. This means that even after making many payments, you could owe more than you did at the beginning of the loan. Negative amortization can occur when an ARM has a payment cap that results in monthly payments not high enough to cover the interest due.

Net Income: Your take-home pay, the amount of money that you receive in your paycheck after taxes and deductions.

No Cash Out Refinance: a refinance of an existing loan only for the amount remaining on the mortgage. The borrower does not get any cash against the equity of the home. Also called a "rate and term refinance."

No Cost Loan: there are many variations of a no cost loan. Generally, it is a loan that does not charge for items such as title insurance, escrow fees, settlement fees, appraisal, recording fees or notary fees. It may also offer no points. This lessens the need for upfront cash during the buying process however no cost loans have a higher interest rate.

Nonperforming Asset: an asset such as a mortgage that is not currently accruing interest or which interest is not being paid.

Note: a legal document obligating a borrower to repay a mortgage loan at a stated interest rate over a specified period of time.

Note Rate: the interest rate stated on a mortgage note.

Notice of Default: a formal written notice to a borrower that there is a default on a loan and that legal action is possible.

Notional Principal Amount: the proposed amount which interest rate swap payments are based but generally not paid or received by either party.

Non-Conforming loan: is a loan that exceeds Fannie Mae's and Freddie Mac's loan limits. Freddie Mac and Fannie Mae loans are referred to as conforming loans.

Notary Public: a person who serves as a public official and certifies the authenticity of required signatures on a document by signing and stamping the document.

O

Offer: indication by a potential buyer of a willingness to purchase a home at a specific price; generally put forth in writing.

Original Principal Balance: the total principal owed on a mortgage prior to any payments being made.

Origination: the process of preparing, submitting, and evaluating a loan application; generally includes a credit check, verification of employment, and a property appraisal.

Origination Fee: the charge for originating a loan; is usually calculated in the form of points and paid at closing. One point equals one percent of the loan amount. On a conventional loan, the loan origination fee is the number of points a borrower pays.

Owner Financing: a home purchase where the seller provides all or part of the financing, acting as a lender.

Ownership: ownership is documented by the deed to a property. The type or form of ownership is important if there is a change in the status of the owners or if the property changes ownership.

Owner's Policy: the insurance policy that protects the buyer from title defects.

P

PITI: Principal, Interest, Taxes, and Insurance: the four elements of a monthly mortgage payment; payments of principal and interest go directly towards repaying the loan while the portion that covers taxes and insurance (homeowner's and mortgage, if applicable) goes into an escrow account to cover the fees when they are due.

PITI Reserves: a cash amount that a borrower must have on hand after making a down payment and paying all closing costs for the purchase of a home. The principal, interest, taxes, and insurance (PITI) reserves must equal the amount that the borrower would have to pay for PITI for a predefined number of months.

PMI: Private Mortgage Insurance; privately-owned companies that offer standard and special affordable mortgage insurance programs for qualified borrowers with down payments of less than 20% of a purchase price.

Partial Claim: a loss mitigation option offered by the FHA that allows a borrower, with help from a lender, to get an interest-free loan from HUD to bring their mortgage payments up to date.

Partial Payment: a payment that is less than the total amount owed on a monthly mortgage payment. Normally, lenders do not accept partial payments. The lender may make exceptions during times of difficulty. Contact your lender prior to the due date if a partial payment is needed.

Payment Cap: a limit on how much an ARM's payment may increase, regardless of how much the interest rate increases.

Payment Change Date: the date when a new monthly payment amount takes effect on an adjustable-rate mortgage (ARM) or a graduated-payment mortgage (GPM). Generally, the payment change date occurs in the month immediately after the interest rate adjustment date.

Payment Due Date: Contract language specifying when payments are due on money borrowed. The due date is always indicated and means that the payment must be received on or before the specified date. Grace periods prior to assessing a late fee or additional interest do not eliminate the responsibility of making payments on time.

Perils: for homeowner's insurance, an event that can damage the property. Homeowner's insurance may cover the property for a wide variety of perils caused by accidents, nature, or people.

Personal Property: any property that is not real property or attached to real property. For example furniture is not attached however a new light fixture would be considered attached and part of the real property.

Planned Unit Development (PUD): a development that is planned, and constructed as one entity. Generally, there are common features in the homes or lots governed by covenants attached to the deed. Most planned developments have common land and facilities owned and managed by the owner's or neighborhood association. Homeowners usually are required to participate in the association via a payment of annual dues.

Points: a point is equal to one percent of the principal amount of your mortgage. For example, if you get a mortgage for $95,000, one point means you pay $950 to the lender. Lenders frequently charge points in both fixed-rate and adjustable-rate mortgages in order to increase the yield on the mortgage and to cover loan closing costs. These points usually are collected at closing and may be paid by the borrower or the home seller, or may be split between them.

Power of Attorney: a legal document that authorizes another person to act on your behalf. A power of attorney can grant complete authority or can be limited to certain acts or certain periods of time or both.

Pre-Approval: a lender commits to lend to a potential borrower a fixed loan amount based on a completed loan application, credit reports, debt, savings and has been reviewed by an underwriter. The commitment remains as long as the borrower still meets the qualification requirements at the time of purchase. This does not guaranty a loan until the property has passed inspections underwriting guidelines.

Predatory Lending: abusive lending practices that include a mortgage loan to someone who does not have the ability to repay. It also pertains to repeated refinancing of a loan charging high interest and fees each time.

Predictive Variables: The variables that are part of the formula comprising elements of a credit-scoring model. These variables are used to predict a borrower's future credit performance.

Preferred Stock: stock that takes priority over common stock with regard to dividends and liquidation rights. Preferred stockholders typically have no voting rights.

Pre-foreclosure Sale: a procedure in which the borrower is allowed to sell a property for an amount less than what is owed on it to avoid a foreclosure. This sale fully satisfies the borrower's debt.

Prepayment: any amount paid to reduce the principal balance of a loan before the due date or payment in full of a mortgage. This can occur with the sale of the property, the pay off the loan in full, or a foreclosure. In each case, full payment occurs before the loan has been fully amortized.

Prepayment Penalty: a provision in some loans that charge a fee to a borrower who pays off a loan before it is due.

Pre-Foreclosure sale: allows a defaulting borrower to sell the mortgaged property to satisfy the loan and avoid foreclosure.

Pre-Qualify: a lender informally determines the maximum amount an individual is eligible to borrow. This is not a guaranty of a loan.

Premium: an amount paid on a regular schedule by a policyholder that maintains insurance coverage.

Prepayment: payment of the mortgage loan before the scheduled due date; may be Subject to a prepayment penalty.

Prepayment Penalty: a fee charged to a homeowner who pays one or more monthly payments before the due date. It can also apply to principal reduction payments.

Prepayment Penalty Mortgage (PPM): a type of mortgage that requires the borrower to pay a penalty for prepayment, partial payment of principal or for repaying the entire loan within a certain time period. A partial payment is generally defined as an amount exceeding 20% of the original principal balance.

Price Range: the high and low amount a buyer is willing to pay for a home.

Prime Rate: the interest rate that banks charge to preferred customers. Changes in the prime rate are publicized in the business media. Prime rate can be used as the basis for adjustable rate mortgages (ARMs) or home equity lines of credit. The prime rate also affects the current interest rates being offered at a particular point in time on fixed mortgages. Changes in the prime rate do not affect the interest on a fixed mortgage.

Principal: the amount of money borrowed to buy a house or the amount of the loan that has not been paid back to the lender. This does not include the interest paid to borrow that money. The principal balance is the amount owed on a loan at any given time. It is the original loan amount minus the total repayments of principal made.

Principal, Interest, Taxes, and Insurance (PITI): the four elements of a monthly mortgage payment; payments of principal and interest go directly towards repaying the loan while the portion that covers taxes and insurance (homeowner's and mortgage, if applicable) goes into an escrow account to cover the fees when they are due.

Private Mortgage Insurance (PMI): insurance purchased by a buyer to protect the lender in the event of default. The cost of mortgage insurance is usually added to the monthly payment. Mortgage insurance is generally maintained until over 20 Percent of the outstanding amount of the loan is paid or for a set period of time, seven years is normal. Mortgage insurance may be available through a government agency, such as the Federal Housing Administration (FHA) or the Veterans Administration (VA), or through private mortgage insurance companies (PMI).

Promissory Note: a written promise to repay a specified amount over a specified period of time.

Property (Fixture and Non-Fixture): in a real estate contract, the property is the land within the legally described boundaries and all permanent structures and fixtures. Ownership of the property confers the legal right to use the property as allowed within the law and within the restrictions of zoning or easements. Fixture property refers to those items permanently attached to the structure, such as carpeting or a ceiling fan, which transfers with the property.

Property Tax: a tax charged by local government and used to fund municipal services such as schools, police, or street maintenance. The amount of property tax is determined locally by a formula, usually based on a percent per $1,000 of assessed value of the property.

Property Tax Deduction: the U.S. tax code allows homeowners to deduct the amount they have paid in property taxes from there total income.

Public Record Information: Court records of events that are a matter of public interest such as credit, bankruptcy, foreclosure and tax liens. The presence of public record information on a credit report is regarded negatively by creditors.

Punch List: a list of items that have not been completed at the time of the final walk through of a newly constructed home.

Purchase Offer: A detailed, written document that makes an offer to purchase a property, and that may be amended several times in the process of negotiations. When signed by all parties involved in the sale, the purchase offer becomes a legally binding contract, sometimes called the Sales Contract.

Q

Quitclaim Deed: a deed transferring ownership of a property but does not make any guarantee of clear title.

R

RESPA: Real Estate Settlement Procedures Act; a law protecting consumers from abuses during the residential real estate purchase and loan process by requiring lenders to disclose all settlement costs, practices, and relationships

Radon: a radioactive gas found in some homes that, if occurring in strong enough concentrations, can cause health problems.

Rate Cap: a limit on an ARM on how much the interest rate or mortgage payment may change. Rate caps limit how much the interest rates can rise or fall on the adjustment dates and over the life of the loan.

Rate Lock: a commitment by a lender to a borrower guaranteeing a specific interest rate over a period of time at a set cost.

Real Estate Agent: an individual who is licensed to negotiate and arrange real estate sales; works for a real estate broker.

Real Estate Mortgage Investment Conduit (REMIC): a security representing an interest in a trust having multiple classes of securities. The securities of each class entitle investors to cash payments structured differently from the payments on the underlying mortgages.

Real Estate Property Tax Deduction: a tax deductible expense reducing a taxpayer's taxable income.

Real Estate Settlement Procedures Act (RESPA): a law protecting consumers from abuses during the residential real estate purchase and loan process by requiring lenders to disclose all settlement costs, practices, and relationships

Real Property: land, including all the natural resources and permanent buildings on it.

REALTOR©: a real estate agent or broker who is a member of the NATIONAL ASSOCIATION OF REALTORS, and its local and state associations.

Recorder: the public official who keeps records of transactions concerning real property. Sometimes known as a "Registrar of Deeds" or "County Clerk."

Recording: the recording in a registrar's office of an executed legal document. These include deeds, mortgages, satisfaction of a mortgage, or an extension of a mortgage making it a part of the public record.

Recording Fees: charges for recording a deed with the appropriate government agency.

Refinancing: paying off one loan by obtaining another; refinancing is generally done to secure better loan terms (like a lower interest rate).

Rehabilitation Mortgage: a mortgage that covers the costs of rehabilitating (repairing or Improving) a property; some rehabilitation mortgages - like the FHA's 203(k) - allow a borrower to roll the costs of rehabilitation and home purchase into one mortgage loan.

Reinstatement Period: a phase of the foreclosure process where the homeowner has an opportunity to stop the foreclosure by paying money that is owed to the lender.

Remaining Balance: the amount of principal that has not yet been repaid.

Remaining Term: the original amortization term minus the number of payments that have been applied.

Repayment plan: an agreement between a lender and a delinquent borrower where the borrower agrees to make additional payments to pay down past due amounts while making regularly scheduled payments.

Return On Average Common Equity: net income available to common stockholders, as a percentage of average common stockholder equity.

Reverse Mortgage (HECM): the reverse mortgage is used by senior homeowners age 62 and older to convert the equity in their home into monthly streams of income and/or a line of credit to be repaid when they no longer occupy the home. A lending institution such as a mortgage lender, bank, credit union or savings and loan association funds the FHA insured loan, commonly known as HECM.

Right of First Refusal: a provision in an agreement that requires the owner of a property to give one party an opportunity to purchase or lease a property before it is offered for sale or lease to others.

Risk Based Capital: an amount of capital needed to offset losses during a ten-year period with adverse circumstances.

Risk Based Pricing: Fee structure used by creditors based on risks of granting credit to a borrower with a poor credit history.

Risk Scoring: an automated way to analyze a credit report verses a manual review. It takes into account late payments, outstanding debt, credit experience, and number of inquiries in an unbiased manner.

S

Sale Leaseback: when a seller deeds property to a buyer for a payment, and the buyer simultaneously leases the property back to the seller.

Second Mortgage: an additional mortgage on property. In case of a default the first mortgage must be paid before the second mortgage.

Second loans are more risky for the lender and usually carry a higher interest rate.

Secondary Mortgage Market: the buying and selling of mortgage loans. Investors purchase residential mortgages originated by lenders, which in turn provides the lenders with capital for additional lending.

Secured Loan: a loan backed by collateral such as property.

Security: the property that will be pledged as collateral for a loan.

Seller Take Back: an agreement where the owner of a property provides second mortgage financing. These are often combined with an assumed mortgage instead of a portion of the seller's equity.

Serious Delinquency: a mortgage that is 90 days or more past due.

Servicer: a business that collects mortgage payments from borrowers and manages the borrower's escrow accounts.

Servicing: the collection of mortgage payments from borrowers and related responsibilities of a loan servicer.

Setback: the distance between a property line and the area where building can take place. Setbacks are used to assure space between buildings and from roads for a many of purposes including drainage and utilities.

Settlement: another name for closing.

Settlement Statement: a document required by the Real Estate Settlement Procedures Act (RESPA). It is an itemized statement of services and charges relating to the closing of a property transfer. The buyer has the right to examine the settlement statement 1 day before the closing. This is called the HUD 1 Settlement Statement.

Special Forbearance: a loss mitigation option where the lender arranges a revised repayment plan for the borrower that may include a temporary reduction or suspension of monthly loan payments.

Stockholders' Equity: the sum of proceeds from the issuance of stock and retained earnings less amounts paid to repurchase common shares.

Stripped MBS (SMBS): securities created by "stripping" or separating the principal and interest payments from the underlying pool of mortgages into two classes of securities, with each receiving a different proportion of the principal and interest payments.

Sub-Prime Loan: "B" Loan or "B" paper with FICO scores from 620 - 659. "C" Loan or "C" Paper with FICO scores typically from 580 to 619. An industry term to used to describe loans with less stringent lending and underwriting terms and conditions. Due to the higher risk, sub-prime loans charge higher interest rates and fees.

Subordinate: to place in a rank of lesser importance or to make one claim secondary to another.

Survey: a property diagram that indicates legal boundaries, easements, encroachments, rights of way, improvement locations, etc. Surveys are conducted by licensed surveyors and are normally required by the lender in order to confirm that the property boundaries and features such as buildings, and easements are correctly described in the legal description of the property.

Sweat Equity: using labor to build or improve a property as part of the down payment.

T

Third Party Origination: a process by which a lender uses another party to completely or partially originate, process, underwrite, close, fund, or package the mortgages it plans to deliver to the secondary mortgage market.

Terms: The period of time and the interest rate agreed upon by the lender and the borrower to repay a loan.

Title: a legal document establishing the right of ownership and is recorded to make it part of the public record. Also known as a Deed.

Title 1: an FHA-insured loan that allows a borrower to make non-luxury improvements (like renovations or repairs) to their home; Title I loans less than $7,500 don't require a property lien.

Title Company: a company that specializes in examining and insuring titles to real estate.

Title Defect: an outstanding claim on a property that limits the ability to sell the property. Also referred to as a cloud on the title.

Title Insurance: insurance that protects the lender against any claims that arise from arguments about ownership of the property; also available for homebuyers. An insurance policy guaranteeing the accuracy of a title search protecting against errors. Most lenders require the buyer to purchase title insurance protecting the lender against loss in the event of a title defect. This charge is included in the closing costs. A policy that protects the buyer from title defects is known as an owner's policy and requires an additional charge.

Title Search: a check of public records to be sure that the seller is the recognized owner of the real estate and that there are no unsettled liens or other claims against the property.

Transfer Agent: a bank or trust company charged with keeping a record of a company's stockholders and canceling and issuing certificates as shares are bought and sold.

Transfer of Ownership: any means by which ownership of a property changes hands. These include purchase of a property, assumption of mortgage debt, exchange of possession of a property via a land sales contract or any other land trust device.

Transfer Taxes: State and local taxes charged for the transfer of real estate. Usually equal to a percentage of the sales price.

Treasury Index: can be used as the basis for adjustable rate mortgages (ARMs) It is based on the results of auctions that the U.S. Treasury holds for its Treasury bills and securities.

Truth-in-Lending: a federal law obligating a lender to give full written disclosure of all fees, terms, and conditions associated with the loan initial period and then adjusts to another rate that lasts for the term of the loan.

Two Step Mortgage: an adjustable-rate mortgage (ARM) that has one interest rate for the first five to seven years of its term and a different interest rate for the remainder of the term.

Trustee: a person who holds or controls property for the benefit of another.

U

Underwriting: the process of analyzing a loan application to determine the amount of risk involved in making the loan; it includes a review of the potential borrower's credit history and a judgment of the property value.

Up Front Charges: the fees charged to homeowners by the lender at the time of closing a mortgage loan. This includes points, broker's fees, insurance, and other charges.

V

VA (Department of Veterans Affairs): a federal agency, which guarantees loans made to veterans; similar to mortgage insurance, a loan guarantee protects lenders against loss that may result from a borrower default.

VA Mortgage: a mortgage guaranteed by the Department of Veterans Affairs (VA).

Variable Expenses: Costs or payments that may vary from month to month, for example, gasoline or food.

Variance: a special exemption of a zoning law to allow the property to be used in a manner different from an existing law.

Vested: a point in time when you may withdraw funds from an investment account, such as a retirement account, without penalty.

W

Walk Through: the final inspection of a property being sold by the buyer to confirm that any contingencies specified in the purchase agreement such as repairs have been completed, fixture and non-fixture property is in place and confirm the electrical, mechanical, and plumbing systems are in working order.

Warranty Deed: a legal document that includes the guarantee the seller is the true owner of the property, has the right to sell the property and there are no claims against the property.

Z

Zoning: local laws established to control the uses of land within a particular area. Zoning laws are used to separate residential land from areas of non-residential use, such as industry or businesses. Zoning ordinances include many provisions governing such things as type of structure, setbacks, lot size, and uses of a building.

Courtesy of HUD

INDEX